D1545075

Theology in Conflict

THEOLOGY IN CONFLICT

Nygren — Barth — Bultmann

by

Gustaf Wingren

Translated by Eric H. Wahlstrom

Muhlenberg Press   Philadelphia, Pa.

Table of Contents

Introduction

All theologians work according to a certain method, even those who have not issued a specific methodological program. There are in every case some presuppositions which precede the beginning of the approach to the subject. That which is thus presupposed is what we intend to examine from a definite and well-defined point of view. Our task is, therefore, a critical examination of the currently prominent theology. We assume that the method of working is everywhere a problem, and that it is recognized as such. It is not our intention to add a new and hitherto unused method to those already in use. In the course of our critical analysis certain suggestions in regard to method may well appear. But our essential concern is the critical analysis itself. It is the principal, contemporary theology which continually claims our attention. Consequently, the most influential contemporary theologians—Nygren, Barth and Bultmann—dominate the outline of our presentation.

Presuppositions may, however, be of very different kinds. Even the most simple statement about everyday affairs, when subjected to analysis, is certain to contain a number of unexpressed presuppositions. Theological statements are in general richer in this respect than any others. It is not our purpose to examine all the presuppositions which appear in modern theology. Both the nature of the presuppositions which we intend to examine and the point of view from which we examine them are exactly defined and strictly delimited. The most important part of this introduction is to indicate clearly this nature and this point of view. Consequently, several problems which in themselves might be worthy of study lie outside of the subject which we have chosen.

We must first say a few words about the nature of the presuppositions. The presuppositions in contemporary theology in which we are interested and which claim our entire attention are of two kinds. It will appear, however, that these two are very closely related, and that in each case we are dealing with presuppositions of the same nature. When we separate them and speak, on the one hand, of hermeneutical presuppositions and, on the other hand, of anthropological presuppositions, the division is motivated primarily by technical considerations. The presentation gains in clarity if we approach the presuppositions step by step.

The procedure will be as follows: In the first part we will examine the anthropological presuppositions in the theological systems of Anders Nygren, Karl Barth, and Rudolf Bultmann. In the second part we will deal with the hermeneutical presuppositions in the theological systems of these three theologians. We could, of course, have finished the critical examination of each of these theologians in turn, and thus mixed anthropology and hermeneutics. That would have afforded us certain advantages which we lose on account of this division in our outline. But this procedure provides also certain advantages which are different and more important. In this way we are able to define the anthropological and hermeneutical presuppositions more clearly as in themselves inescapable problems which must be clarified if we are to make any progress in theological study. Furthermore, by this disposition of the subject we break through the boundaries of modern theological tendencies. This is in itself an advantage. One of the greatest difficulties in theological work in our day is the fact that the boundaries between different theological systems are geographical, i.e., boundaries between countries.

We must here indicate what we mean by anthropological and hermeneutical presuppositions. Every theology presupposes something about how the New Testament should be read and what it is. We can read the New Testament as the precipitate of the religious faith of the early church, or as writings which grew out of an originally oral preaching, etc. At first sight these variations appear to differ very slightly from one another, but since they involve an elemental factor—the way in which a certain writing is read—even a very slight variation at the outset will have a tremendous influence on the results as the theological work progresses. It yields a harvest, thirtyfold, sixtyfold, and hundredfold. We are concerned here with a theological attitude toward the historical roots of the Christian faith. Something is presupposed in regard to primitive Christianity, Jesus, and the biblical writings. This we call here "hermeneutical presuppositions."

Every theology also presupposes a conception about man and his situation as this Word which we try to interpret confronts him. It is obvious that we presuppose something about man in the early church, or in the medieval period, or in the time of the Reformation. But every theology presupposes something about man in general, about contemporary man. This is not obvious and sometimes not even admitted. On the contrary we would rather hide this from ourselves as theologians and from those who read our theological production. In modern theology there appears at times a direct criticism of the idea that theology must presuppose a certain anthropology. But an analysis will disclose that something is always presupposed; for example, that man apart from scripture has no knowledge of God and his will, or that the spiritual or cultural life as a whole rests on no kind of foundation, or that man always stands in the throes of decision. By the acceptance of such presuppositions a foundation has already been established —negatively or positively. The hermeneutical presuppositions with which we approach our task of interpreting "Christianity," "the Word," or "the kerygma," correspond to other presuppositions concerning man, the cultural life, and humanity. In our presentation we call these latter "anthropological presuppositions." We attempt, therefore, purposely to isolate anthropology and hermeneutics and to confine our study to these two subjects. Their inner connection will become apparent in the analysis of the three theologians we have chosen to discuss.

It would, of course, be possible to imagine a kind of theology which would not be *so* completely tied down to hermeneutics and anthropology as modern theology actually is. But in regard to hermeneutics it is remarkable how often it happens that a line of theological reasoning, which makes no pretense of being an interpretation of scripture, nevertheless at critical points employs arguments from "the teaching of Jesus," "the New Testament point of view," etc. The three theologians whom we discuss accept such arguments on principle and deliberately use them as the foundation of their theological systems. But even other theologians who would deny that theology is interpretation of scripture and understand the theological task differently nevertheless show that they presuppose a certain concrete interpretation of primitive Christianity, or of the historical Jesus. In regard to anthropology it becomes even more obvious how common these hidden presuppositions are. Such terms as "faith" and "salvation" occur inevitably in all theological discussions, and the sense in which the content of these terms is understood implies a definite anthropology.

We must at this point also clarify the point of view from which we intend to examine critically the presuppositions found in modern theology. This point of view can be fixed and defined quite accurately. We ask: Are these presuppositions valid on the basis of the Bible and specifically the New Testament? The more clearly we define the point of view from which for the moment a certain problem is approached, the clearer it generally becomes that other approaches also could be used. Since many modern theologians have deliberately accepted certain concrete philosophical tendencies (this is true also of the three here discussed), it might seem proper to examine their theology from a philosophical viewpoint. Such a study might well be undertaken, but it is not our task here.

Even an immanent criticism of Barth, Nygren, and Bultmann will reveal that the purely theological question which we have raised is of far greater significance than the philosophical. To criticize these theologians from the point of view of scripture is to criticize them on the basis of their own principles, i.e., their most central principles. A philosophical criticism in regard to them would be rather peripheral. This is true of all three—even of Bultmann, though he is the one most open to attack from a philosophical point of view. But even if we do not one-sidedly insist that these men must be criticized within their own system, but look at the whole problem in general and permit points of view foreign to these theologians, the critical problem that we have posed is nevertheless the most important theological question that can be raised. A theology which has given up the task of interpreting "Christianity," "the Word," "revelation," (using these words in their broadest sense) is no longer theology.

We must point out at once that we do not consistently adhere to a purely immanent criticism in the course of this study. To speak of the contrast between *Gott* and *Mensch* in Karl Barth under the caption of anthropology does not agree with Barth's own usage. It is also foreign to him to analyze the concept of *das Wort* under the caption of hermeneutics. The situation is the same when we discuss Anders Nygren's critical philosophy of religion under anthropology and his motif research under hermeneutics. Our terminology is most appropriate in the case of Bultmann, although our criticism of him will possibly be more severe than of the other two. Our terminology, which is to some extent *imposed* upon them, is nevertheless chosen deliberately, just as we have chosen to divide the study into two parts. In both of these parts, the terminology and the outline, there are essential results derived from our own thesis concerning the definition of the task of theology. We do not intend to produce a purely descriptive presentation of the theology of these three authors. Nor are we interested in a genetic study. Their points of view are regarded as generally well known. There are no exhaustive references, and the footnotes have been kept at a minimum.[1] The emphasis is on a continuous and thoroughgoing critical reasoning, the criticism being sometimes immanent, sometimes transcendent. How the criticism is carried through insofar as it is transcendent is explained in the fourth chapter of each part: "Review and Perspective," and "Retrospect and Conclusion."

But we must still add something more regarding the point of view from which we make our critical examination of these presuppositions. We start with the fact that in all this modern theological writing something is presupposed: on the one hand,

---

[1] The number of footnotes has been still further reduced in the translation, since the books and articles in Swedish which are cited in the text are not readily available to English readers. (Translator's note.)

concerning the right way of reading scripture; and, on the other hand, concerning the situation of man as he is confronted with the content of scripture. It is presuppositions of this nature that we intend to expose in the modern theological material with which we are dealing. Afterwards the question arises: Can these presuppositions which we find in this material be criticized on the basis of scripture itself? We expect, therefore, a *conflict*. The theologian may have a view of the sources which is not historically accurate. He may also be working with a conception of man's situation relative to the Word which is different from the conception which the biblical writings themselves represent. There may be a conflict here. We must, therefore, define more closely what our interest is in regard to such an eventual conflict.

In the first place, the conflict may be open, deliberate, and expressed. The modern writer says: I note this element in the Bible, but I deny and reject it. We meet this type of conflict in all three of the theologians whom we examine. Conflicts of this nature are found most frequently in Bultmann, not so often in Barth and Nygren. But it is important to note that they do occur even in the latter two. We may, for instance, point to Nygren's attitude to the idea of Agape in the Gospel of John as he sets it forth in *Agape and Eros*[2]; and to Barth's rather supercilious refusal to see any significance in the fall of the angels as that is presented in Jude 6 and II Pet. 2:4.[3] But we are not vitally interested here in this type of conflict. When any one of these three theologians rejects some peripheral part of scripture, or a certain detail in a specific writing, he does so in order to preserve and enhance that which, ac-

[2] A. Nygren, *Agape and Eros*, trans. Philip S. Watson (Philadelphia: Westminster Press, 1953), p. 151 ff.
[3] *Die kirchliche Dogmatik* III:3 (1950), p. 622 ff.

cording to his view, is essential in the Bible. All three desire to explain, interpret, and elucidate the genuine New Testament and early Christian message. It often happens that it becomes necessary to criticize a certain aspect of a document in order to accentuate its central meaning. Such a rejection of an element in the document is not a real conflict, provided that it cannot be shown, contrary to the interpreter's opinion, that the part rejected is an *essential* element. Such a protest is not a hidden presupposition within the theological system; it is an open and expressed assertion. This type of conflict with scripture lies outside of our chief concern.

In the second place, the conflict may be caused by insufficient historical insight on the part of the modern theologian. A modern writer aims to present a certain New Testament situation as it really is. But there may nevertheless be a discrepancy between his statements and scripture because he has erroneous information about the situation which he describes. A more exact historical research may be able to give a different and more convincing presentation of the meaning of scripture on this particular point. We can find this type of conflict with biblical statements in all three of the theologians under discussion. Their writings are subject to exegetical discussion, and the critics have not accepted all of their results as historically accurate. Thus objections have been raised against Bultmann's peculiar way of parceling out the various historical factors involved in the development of the kerygma, especially his description of the teaching of Jesus, of the primitive church, and of the Hellenistic congregations before Paul. Similarly Barth's exegesis of Gen. 1-2 and Nygren's conception of the doctrine of the two ages and the relationship between the Testaments have met with critical opposition. But we have very little interest in this type of conflict. If the error can be corrected by more exact historical information and the work continued as planned, such an exegetical mistake is of no interest to us even if it should be both flagrant and extensive. In that case the correction does not touch the way of approach or the theological method. The *method* would then be correct, since it would be possible to continue working along the same line after the correction has been made. Consequently we are not interested in this type of conflict with scripture.

In the third place, the conflict may be caused by the method of research. In that case the author wants to interpret the biblical content, not set it aside. But he encounters a certain resistance. An examination of the biblical content reveals that there is a tension between essential parts of the biblical material and the modern theological interpretation. But he cannot correct the interpretation and then continue the work because the correction strikes at the very conception or grasp of the subject, the method of the whole work, the very first presuppositions with which he started his investigation. If the correction demanded on the basis of the Bible were to be taken seriously, everything that had been achieved so far would have to be destroyed and the work begun anew. The conflict is fundamental. In the new building a number of stones and other material that have been laboriously gathered together might be used, but the blueprint could not be followed.

It is this blueprint for which we are continually hunting when we begin to analyze these three theologians. We call attention to their grasp of their subject, the structure which they project before they begin to build, i.e., before they begin to argue, marshal their material, etc. In regard to this blueprint we ask the same questions of all three: What are the anthropological presuppositions? What are the hermeneutical presuppositions? Do these fundamental presuppositions stand in a real and evi dent conflict with the biblical material which these theologians aim to interpret? How can we define this fundamental conflict in the case of each of these men? Our whole interest is concentrated on this problem in the exposition which follows. Any other problems in connection with these three theologians we regard as of lesser importance and leave them purposely out of consideration.

It should be emphasized here that among the problems which we set aside there are many also of a historical nature, not only and not chiefly philosophical. Barth, Bultmann, and Nygren operate with a definite interpretation of Luther. Each one has his own interpretation of him, and this interpretation of Luther is in each case of very great importance for their whole theological system. But in our presentation we touch on Luther only insofar as he may be regarded as the representative of a specific *biblical* line of thought. We have no direct interest in Luther, nor in the way he has been interpreted by our three theologians. We could also mention a number of other historical problems; for instance, Barth's and Nygren's different interpretation of Schleiermacher, which is an important element in both. But the main point is that all these are regarded in our presentation as peripheral problems to which we do not devote an independent analysis. They are considered only insofar as they impinge on the chief problem that we have to investigate.

It is impossible to suggest in advance any concrete example of how such a fundamental conflict appears. We do not become aware of this conflict by examining specific points in the work of a theologian. We must first work through the various points, and then take a bird's-eye view of the system as a whole, the plan, the total structure which determines every single part, and especially determines the place each part is to be given. In our work here, therefore, we have to move continually toward the modern interpretation and then away from it. We have to determine the content of what each one of our authors has to say on certain crucial points. Then we have to ask whether what they say is in conflict with the biblical material. And we have to try to find the point in the very conception of their work which explains the conflict.

We proceed here on the assumption that such elements which disturb the comprehension of the biblical material that is to be interpreted ought to be removed. This, our own presupposition, is not necessarily obvious. It could be argued that one aspect in a theology which makes a correct interpretation of scripture difficult is merely a minor mistake in this theology, especially if in recompense certain other more important results may be achieved in consequence of using this method of work. This assumption that any factors which disturb the apprehension of the biblical material ought to be removed indicates that we are to a large extent influenced by the three theologians who are the object of our study: Barth, Nygren and Bultmann. These three would agree in principle that the removal of such factors is desirable. But they mean different things when they agree to this.

We may note that there are theologians who would not agree to this thesis. To such theologians we pay no attention here. Our choice of and concentration on these three is a measure of the influence which they have exerted; and our own assumption—that disturbing factors must be removed—indicates even more strongly our dependence upon them. We have not, of course, made this selection in order to enhance something common to Barth, Bultmann, and Nygren which we might think valuable for further theological study. We have selected them simply because they are the most influential and representative when the question concerning the definition of the task of theology is under discussion. There are theological programs which are of great theoretical interest, although they have no great practical significance except for those who have worked them out. They do not influence the current theological work. In a historical situation different from the present it might have been more to the point to analyze the work of those who are now voices in the wilderness. We have chosen, however, to analyze those who at present have put their stamp on theological research. That in doing so we at the same time become dependent upon them is obvious.

In establishing the thesis that whatever element in the approach prevents a correct understanding of the material must be removed we touch upon a difficult problem which must be clarified. No one would deny that it is a flaw in a scientific historical work if the method itself is such that it prevents a correct understanding of the material at certain important points. It is a truism that in such a case we should remove the hindrance and improve the method. But if we assume that the material studied is an old law which is still in force, new problems arise. The legal historian may refine the historical analysis and explain his material more adequately than his predecessors have been able to do. If, however, the question is raised concerning what this law means now, how its meaning is to be related to present social factors which were unknown when the law was written, new types of problems arise. But since the law is still in force, these new problems are fully legitimate problems of interpretation. The purely historical results are of immediate significance for the solution of these problems. But new circumstances have appeared which must be taken into consideration in interpreting the text. It might easily be shown that the new situations may have an adverse influence on the interpretation of the law. It is not impossible to arrive finally at an interpretation which diverges from both the letter and the meaning of the law. It is proper, therefore, to subject current interpretations to critical analysis. But in the nature of the case the critical problem cannot then be regarded as a purely historical problem of jurisprudence.

Theology encounters in the text of the Bible difficulties which are to some extent akin to the problems of interpreting the law as here indicated. The results of exegesis have immediate significance for all interpretation of the Bible. But theology must also take into consideration that the Christian faith is *now* alive, and that the word of scripture means something for this present, living Christian faith, although it is separated by centuries from the time when the Word was written, and although the particular conditions of the twentieth century are not mentioned in the Bible. There are many current interpretations of the Bible, and undoubtedly some of them are false. It is proper, therefore, to subject current interpretations to critical analysis. Anyone who maintains that the critical problem can be solved by a purely historical exegesis indicates that he does not realize the full extent of the problem. Exegesis can make important contributions, but it cannot by itself solve the critical problem without ceasing to be purely historical exegesis. At this point it is convenient to take one of Bultmann's arguments as an illustration. He conceives of the critical problem in the widest sense, and he expresses the opinion that a solution requires the combined efforts of a whole generation of theologians. It is also clear that according to him all theological disciplines have their special share in this work.[4]

Bultmann's point of departure is that the New Testament

[4] R. Bultmann, "New Testament and Mythology," in *Kerygma and Myth*, ed. Hans Werner Bartsch, trans. Reginald H. Fuller (New York: Macmillan Co., 1954), p. 15.

kerygma is a gospel, and that it is not rightly understood if it is conceived of as something else than gospel. When it is rightly understood, the gospel strikes the listener as an obvious *skandalon*, an offense; the offense namely that righteousness is a gift bestowed upon man, not something that is obtained by man's own efforts. According to the New Testament kerygma the righteousness thus bestowed upon man rests upon God's act in the death and resurrection of Christ. It seems to be clear that the resurrection in the New Testament is conceived of as a bodily resurrection. When the gospel is preached *now* in this unchanged, ancient form, it does contain an offense, but this offense is quite different from the original, real offense of the gospel. Now the offense consists in the proclamation asserting something which is contrary to science. When a man now listens to this proclamation, he is not urged to receive a gift which denies his own righteousness—this offense belongs to the gospel and must always be retained—but he is expected to achieve an intellectual assent to a proposition which is highly problematical in view of our scientific knowledge.

In other words, he is asked to make a typical effort, to present a typical "work." But in this way the gospel is transformed into its opposite; it does not offer righteousness as a gift but as a reward for believing something that is intellectually improbable. This shift is caused by the fact that modern natural science has come in between the time the New Testament was written and the time when we now listen to its message. If the original offense which was connected with the gift of righteousness is to be understood now, the false, intellectual offense must be removed. But this means that we must reject something of the peripheral in the New Testament in order that the central element might be given its rightful place. In Bultmann's case it is not a question of a mechanical selection of various equal items, i.e., reject some, accept something else. There is a consistent unity in his method of interpretation. He rejects a peripheral element *in order* to be able to throw light on that which is central. The miracles have to step aside for the gospel.

But how does the matter stand if by the elimination of the bodily resurrection of Christ an essential element of the gospel itself might be lost? Karl Barth has urged this against Bultmann with very good arguments. How are we to decide? As always when it is a question between essentials and nonessentials a choice has to be made. The scriptures as historically given must not be set aside. The cultural and spiritual situation of the man who listens must not be ignored. None of the three theologians whom we consider here has neglected these two factors. They are working continually in contact with the biblical material. At the same time they hold a certain conception of man as he is confronted with the message of scripture. But this dichotomy is exactly what we have here called hermeneutics and anthropology.

When we now consider these two aspects from a different point of view than before, it might seem that they stand in tension with one another rather than in inner harmony. It is really true that in a living theology which has escaped the perils of sterility there is a tension between these two: the content of scripture clashes with the accepted world view and at the same time seeks points of contact in this view in order to become comprehensible. But as the work of interpretation progresses and the decisions are finally made, they are made in such a way that the two factors harmonize one with the other. Bultmann thus arrives in his interpretation at a close inner harmony between his exegesis of the New Testament documents and his philosophical analysis of human existence.

Barth comes to his opposite position with a similar harmony between his definition of *das Wort* and its content and a corresponding, negative conception of man confronted with the Word. In Nygren's work there is a similar frictionless unity. The fundamental motif which emerges out of the historical analysis of Christianity as given is found to be the answer to the fundamental question which has been shown in the philosophical analysis to be one of humanity's inevitable questions.

As this point we proceed to the task of describing and critically examining this inner unity between anthropology and hermeneutics in each of these three authors.[5]

[5] The discussion of each of these three theologians demands to some extent, at least momentarily, that we accept their specific terminology. To be sure, our purpose is to break up and criticize their fundamental point of view. But we can accomplish this only by going into the house they have built and speaking their language. Since we have to deal here with three different "houses" and three different sets of terminology, our criticism will have to employ different terms in each of the three parts. This change in terminology is naturally a defect, but it is in some measure compensated for by the unity in the outline.

PART ONE

ANTHROPOLOGICAL PRESUPPOSITIONS

CHAPTER ONE

Nygren's Critical Philosophy of Religion

The foremost scholarly contribution by Anders Nygren belongs to the realm of the history of ideas. However, before he began any work in that field, he had busied himself for more than a decade with philosophical problems, and had published a number of books which unfortunately even to this day are practically unknown outside of the Scandinavian countries. Our attention in this chapter is directed principally to these earlier works.

In two works published in 1921, "The Fundamental Problem in Philosophy of Religion," and *Religious A Priori*,[1] Nygren sought to define the task of a critical philosophy of religion and also attempted to solve the problem thus formulated. Philosophy of religion has to determine whether religion is an a priori form of life. It has to examine whether the claim of religion to be an objective experience is valid. Here objectivity does not mean correspondence with an object. There is no transcendent reality available to which the conceptions of faith can be compared. Philosophy of religion must remain within the subjective realm and find the basis on which it can differentiate between objectivity and subjectivity in an immanent criterion within the subjective sphere. It is true that religion itself regards its object as a transcendent reality. But philosophy of religion views religion as remaining in principle within

[1] A. Nygren, "Det religionsfilosofiska grundproblemet," in *Biblefor-skaren*, XXXVI (1919), 290-313, and XXXVIII (1921), 11-39, 88-103. A. Nygren, *Religiöst a priori* (Lund, 1921).

the sphere of the subject. The question about a knowable transcendent reality is here left open and unanswered. The validity of the claim made by religion can be tested anyway. A phenomenon is valid if it is a necessary and indispensable form of life, i.e., if its special value is a fundamental value which cannot be realized in any other form of life.

The idea of a "a fundamental value" incorporates religion in "a system of universally valid values." Knowledge represents one fundamental value, ethics a second, and aesthetics a third. The good is something unique, something *sui generis*, which cannot be derived from the true or the beautiful. We can formulate Nygren's question in *Religious A Priori* thus: Has religion an independent value beside these more generally recognized values (knowledge, aesthetics, etc.), or can it be traced back to one of these others? The answer to this question is found in a process of reasoning in which he first differentiates religion from aesthetics, knowledge, and ethics, and then establishes a definite relationship between religion on the one hand and knowledge, aesthetics, and ethics on the other. Religion must be differentiated from the other three because it must be something unique and independent. But it is not enough that it is different, it must also have validity, and in his argument for the validity of religion he relates it in a definite way to knowledge, ethics, and aesthetics. A phenomenon is valid if it is necessary and indispensable, and this means necessary and indispensable for the others. If we can prove that something must be valid in order that in general anything might be valid, we have, according to Nygren, shown the validity of that which was originally questioned.[2] There is here no attempt to reason about an object.

---

[2] "That which must be valid in order that experience as a whole shall be possible is necessarily and universally valid and is therefore a priori.

4

Nygren follows Kant, but he never maintains that he entirely reproduces his line of thinking as that way of thinking was developed in the practical application.[3] It is the Kantian critical attempt which Nygren wishes to preserve. What Nygren calls "the transcendental deduction of the fundamental category of religion" is a fairly simple and essentially negative reasoning. There is no demonstration of any reality, nor of the truth of the content of any religious statement. The typical formula is as follows: *If* this and that are not valid, then it is meaningless to talk about anything at all as valid; therefore this and that must be valid. "If we can prove that one thing must be valid if we are to speak of validity at all, then we have arrived at a measure of validity for this which cannot be surpassed. The transcendental deduction can best be compared to a negative proof. It seeks to prove that no validity and no experience can exist unless this axiom is acknowledged."[4]

This "other" which would lose all validity unless the "X" in question is valid is "the system of culture." If "X" is religion, the system of culture is knowledge, aesthetics, ethics. The task is "to show that religion stands in a necessary connection with the system of culture insofar as this system in its entirety rests on presuppositions which are realized only in religion."[5] We must go beyond the cultural values in order

This is the transcendental method described in its briefest form. In order to show that a certain knowledge is a priori it must be proved that without the presupposition of its validity no experience is possible." *Religious A Priori, op. cit.*, p. 110. This is primarily a description of Kant's transcendental method, but on this point the description of Kant reflects Nygren's own standpoint.

[3] Nygren attempts, on the basis of Kantian philosophy, to establish the validity of religion. Consequently such terms as a priori, category, transcendental, etc., must be understood in the sense of Kantian critical philosophy. (Translator's note.)

[4] *Religious A Priori, op. cit.*, p. 209.

[5] *Ibid.*, p. 237.

to see on what conditions anything may be accepted as true, good, or beautiful.

In the book, *Religious A Priori*, it sometimes appears as if religion occupied a unique position, as if it alone were the foundation of the system of culture. But this is probably not Nygren's real meaning. It lies in the nature of the problem that the subject whose validity is to be tested must be shown as being the condition for the validity of the other values. If the validity of aesthetics were questioned, aesthetics would assume the same position as religion does in *Religious A Priori*, since in that case it must be demonstrated that aesthetics is essential for the system of culture, i.e., for knowledge, ethics and religion. The validity of the other forms of culture is presupposed hypothetically in every instance.[6]

This is Nygren's program. Its development is a brief argumentation occupying four pages in *Religious A Priori*. The deduction of the fundamental category of religion is arrived at by showing that eternity is presupposed as soon as the good, the true and the beautiful are mentioned. Eternity is presupposed in the whole system of culture. But this eternity is only assumed in such cultural forms as knowledge, ethics and aesthetics. In religion this presupposition is realized, and only there. The category of eternity is the transcendent, fundamental category of religion. The various historical religions

[6] A. Nygren, *Filosofisk och kristen etik (Philosophical and Christian Ethics)* (Stockholm, 1923), p. 148. "Of what kind this 'other' is for whose validity the primary validity is a necessary presupposition has no influence on the sense in which the latter is valid. 'The other' may be knowledge, moral behavior, a religious experience, or anything else. In any case we arrive at the primary validity in the same way, namely by showing that the primary validity is a transcendental presupposition for the 'other.' This is the only way in which the reality of the primary validity can be demonstrated." This quotation occurs in a context where all primary validity is shown to be "colorless," "indifferent," but it is signficant also for the question we are discussing here.

each give their own unique answer to the question of eternity. What the other forms of culture need, unless they are to be without foundation, religion promises to give. Here the end of the philosophical argument is reached. Religion is "necessary, universal and inseparable from the essence of man." [7] This goal was posited from the beginning as the final point of the philosophical argument. What was to be proved was the idealistic necessity of religion; namely, that religion is an essential and integrating factor in consciousness without which consciousness cannot be regarded as perfected, but must be described as to some extent retarded or stunted.[8] The argument is conducted throughout in such a way that the objectivity and validity of religion is upheld without ever using any other criteria than "consciousness" or "the cultural life." Religion is incorporated as a necessary part into the cultural life of humanity.

We are not concerned here with the question whether this transcendental deduction of the fundamental category of religion is philosophically tenable. The most comprehensive philosophical criticism of Nygren's argument is even today the article by Einar Tegen in *Bibelforskaren, (The Student of the Bible)* (1922-23).[9]

[7] *Religious A Priori, op. cit.,* p. 241. Nygren continues: "As surely as man's ascent from nature to a cultural status is an essential progress for man, so also religion is an integrating factor in a real human life."

[8] *Ibid.,* p. 10. After arriving at this goal of philosophy of religion a new task begins: the study of the answer to the question of eternity given by each of the existing religions. This is the task of theology. Theology depends entirely on the fundamental validity which philosophy of religion has established for it by anchoring religion in "consciousness" or in "the system of culture."

[9] Tegen asks two questions: 1) Can validity be separated from the conceptions of an object and of reality? 2) Is the "eternity" presupposed in knowledge, aesthetics, and ethics in any sense related to the eternity with which religion is concerned?

But not even Tegen's criticism has reached the heart of the argument. The religious propositions are said to be valid, but this validity does not mean anything positive to Nygren. The only thing that is valid is religion as a form of experience, but this form is empty and devoid of content. The content lies in the concrete, historical religions where an answer to the question of eternity is given. Philosophy of religion has established only that it is meaningful and legitimate to *ask* about eternity. All the concrete answers of the different religions, in spite of their contradictions, share and share alike in this validity. The same is true in regard to ethics. Philosophical ethics proves that the ethical question is an autonomous question, but it cannot say about any answer or any ethical proposition that they are right. All ethical affirmations, by virtue of their being ethical, i.e., in that they affirm something as good, are equally valid. But this implies that validity does not mean anything. In the theoretical sphere it is possible to accept or reject some of the historically given propositions. There we can distinguish between valid and invalid propositions among the great mass of historically given propositions. But in the ethical and religious spheres of experience no choice can be made on a scientific basis. Each individual must make his own personal choice. But everything from which he makes his choice is valid, for it is either ethical or religious. Thus nothing is really valid except the choice. The choice is necessary because the question is inescapable.

It is difficult to discover this trend as long as we confine our study to "The Fundamental Problem in Philosophy of Religion," and *Religious A Priori*. In these early works Nygren's views have not arrived at a definite pattern. He thinks here in a "pre-critical" or, possibly better, "pre-Lundensian" manner. There is in these earlier works a suggestion that far

8

off in the uttermost extension of religious-philosophical thinking we can anticipate a theology which will provide "the theological proof of the truth" of Christianity, i.e., of one of the
historical religions. When philosophy of religion has established the objective reality of the universal religious value, it
becomes the task of theology "to deal with the question of the
objective reality of a given religion such as Christianity, or
of the validity of its claim to transcendence." It is probable
that Nygren is here influenced by Carl Stange and Johannes
Wendland, who have expressed similar ideas, and have influenced Nygren's thought in his early works.[10] But it is clear
that any concern about "the question of truth" in theology
is very quickly and radically eliminated from Nygren's view.
Already in 1923, when *Philosophical and Christian Ethics* was
published, the elimination was complete. The task of theology
is to *describe* Christianity, to present this historically given
religion (and this historically given ethos) in a purely descriptive manner. The question about the truth of Christianity cannot be raised by scientific theology, and much less be answered.

In the original effort in 1921 "the validity" of religion was
a step on the way toward the "truth" of Christianity. We
could then assume that validity would mean something positive.
When Nygren's system has become stablilized, the "validity"
of religion is a step on the way to a correct description of the
"fundamental motif" in the various religions, among which
Christianity is just one, one among many. All these fundamental motifs are valid, and from a scientific point of view all
are equally true. Then "validity" has no positive meaning. The
whole system of critical, philosophical reasoning which leads

---

[10] J. Wendland, *Die Stellung der Religion im Geistesleben, Beitr. z.
Ford. Christ. Theol.*, 25.2 (1920), p. 12 ff. C. Stange, *Christentum und
moderne Weltanshauung* I (2 Aufl., 1913), p. 114 ff.

up to the conception of the task given to theology, and which is conducted in order to guarantee the scientific character of this conception, now has only the function to eliminate all theoretical criticism and to reject all apologetic defense of the contents of faith.

The religious question is an independent question, and so is the ethical. Scientific study can never help or destroy a religion or an ethos. These answers to the questions of eternity or fellowship are at hand—we simply meet them as actual convictions. The only task of scientific scholarship is simply to describe them correctly. Philosophy of religion and philosophical ethics have done enough when they have demonstrated that there are questions which are essential without being scientific. The plurality of questions is the only thing which critical philosophy is able to demonstrate. This is sufficient for theology. Now theology knows what its task is: to describe as accurately as possible the answer of Christianity to a couple of eternal, unscientific, but inescapable questions; the question about the eternal, or communion with God; and the question about the good, or human fellowship. The task of systematic theology is to characterize these answers, nothing else. It is necessary to avoid all problems which would lead beyond the purely descriptive and characterizing task.

Nygren's mature system appears most clearly in *Philosophical and Christian Ethics*. Here no transcendental deduction of the fundamental category of ethics appears. Here he simply defines the purpose of two scientific disciplines: philosophical and theological ethics. Philosophical ethics has to establish the formal categories that are valid for moral experience. From this empty pattern no specific ethical "duties" can be derived. Nygren suggests that the formal and fundamental category in ethics is fellowship. But this means simply that ethics is concerned with the question of fellowship. Then the "answers" come and affirm something of what constitutes the right and proper forms of fellowship. But these answers simply demand a personal decision. We cannot scientifically support any of them. Christianity gives one answer. Love, Agape, is to govern human fellowship. We can *describe* this Christian content; we can "scientifically determine the significance of this ideal." This is the task of theological ethics. When the investigation began, the two scholarly disciplines appeared rather perplexed, but now they have each received their proper sphere of work.

The result of Nygren's philosophical argumentation is that theology becomes a description of Christianity. This is the final result of the philosophical reasoning. Faith itself finds no support in philosophy of religion, and faith does not need any. The moral conviction receives no support from philosophical ethics, and an ethos does not need any such support. What happens is that scientific theology is given a clearly defined task and is directed to a definite material, viz., Christianity. *Nygren's critical philosophy of religion and his motif research are inseparably connected.* A philosophical appraisal which separates his earlier critical works from his later works in motif research and history of ideas fails to reach the heart and center of his system. "A fundamental motif" is an historical answer to a fundamental question of categorical nature. "The question is philosophically formulated, the answer must be found in the given historical reality. . . . What the fundamental motif is in any particular outlook can be determined only by immediate observation of its appearance in history, and this process involves the same conditions as are found in any other historical investigation." [11] Nygren's historical work, *Agape*

[11] A. Nygren, *Filosofi och motivforskning (Philosophy and Motif Research)* (Stockholm, 1940), p. 44.

and Eros, begins with a definition of the concept of "a fundamental motif" which clearly connects this later historical work with the critical and philosophical production of an earlier period. The Lundensian, historically oriented systematic theology with its concentration on an exact description of various views (Luther research, Orthodoxy, etc.) is the mature fruit of Nygren's purely philosophical, formal, and abstract reasoning begun in his earlier works.

We will have opportunity to examine Nygren's whole system when we deal with his motif research in the chapter on the hermeneutical presuppositions. Here we pass this aspect by and concentrate our attention on the anthropological presuppositions which are inherent in his philosophical and critical approach.

Every area of experience is supposed to be something *sui generis.* Its special question cannot be asked in any other context. In that case it is strange that the question of the True appears as a fundamental question in only one particular context. It is eliminated from the other areas of experience. Truth becomes a category beside other categories. It is impossible to follow this line of reasoning to the end without coming to the conclusion that the human consciousness is productive in the three other areas of experience: aesthetics, ethics, and religion. It is true that afterwards, when we encounter religious and ethical convictions in motif research, these do not present themselves as mere products of the human consciousness. God, not man, is the center in faith. Since the theologian is concerned with pure description, he must describe faith as it really is, i.e., theocentric. But this whole theological description is a description of statements of faith. All the sources are read as containing propositions in which men's faith has been formulated. It should be noted that the statements of both Platonism and ancient Christianity are expressions of faith. These two clash, to be sure, because they represent two diametrically opposed motifs. But these two fundamental motifs are answers to "fundamental questions of categorical nature." None of them are true, and none are false. When you approach them, you regard them as products of the human consciousness.

It would have been possible to define the theoretical context differently without using the word "true" as a characteristic. The emphasis could have been placed on the fact that propositions of knowledge have no relationship to the subject expressing them, while ethical, aesthetic and religious statements invariably are characterized by such a connection. This would not have weakened the demand which is placed on scientific knowledge. But the word "truth" would in that case not have been used as a characteristic of one special context of meaning. It would naturally not have been used to describe the uniqueness of any of the other three fundamental questions. The system would have been open. Now on the contrary the system is closed. A certain number of productive forms of culture which are regarded as expressions of the human consciousness have been added to knowledge, described in positivistic terms.

The problem is whether it is possible for a systematic theology so conceived to pass from philosophy to the theological description of Christianity without bringing along something of the content of the view of "religion" and "ethics" which was imposed on them from the beginning; or, whether this initial point of view enters also into theology itself, into the description of the faith which is to be described, namely the Christian faith. If the latter happens, it is already clear that the description becomes historically incorrect. This is our chief problem, the only point of view from which we will examine the different theological methods. We return to this problem when we examine the historical description in the section dealing with motif research.

At present when we are concerned with the anthropological —not the hermeneutical—presuppositions, another point is of far greater interest. We can understand this other point best if we notice the tasks which Nygren assigns to dogmatics and theological ethics. Systematic theology is traditionally divided into these two disciplines. Nygren "establishes" these two by prefacing them with two critical and philosophical disciplines. Philosophy of religion defines the task of dogmatics. It establishes the categorical and fundamental question for all religion. This question is empty and formal. The answers are found in history where the different existing religions struggle against one another. Dogmatics presents one answer, that of Christianity, in an analysis free from every kind of valuation. Philosophical ethics defines the task of theological ethics. It establishes the categorical and fundamental question for all ethics. This question is also empty and formal. The answers are found in history where the existing types of ethos struggle with one another.

Theological ethics presents one of these answers, that of Christianity, in an analysis free from every kind of valuation. Both of these Christian answers can be comprehended in one word: Agape.[12] Consequently the fundamental motif in Christianity is Agape, which is to be elucidated on the basis of the Christian sources in both dogmatics and theological ethics. The power that brings man into relationship with God is God's own forgiving love, God's Agape. The power that governs the Christian ethos and determines the Christian's relationship to and fellowship with his fellow men is self-giving love, man's

[12] *Agape and Eros, op. cit.,* p. 47.

14

Agape toward his neighbor. Man's Agape toward his neighbor has its source in God's Agape to mankind. The Christian ethos derives from the Christian faith. Theological ethics has to deal only with this ethos derived from faith.

The gospel is the message about God's love, which therefore becomes the Christian answer to the categorical and fundamental question of religion. And the ethos which derives from faith in God's love becomes the center in the description of the Christian answer to the categorical and fundamental question of ethics. It is important to understand clearly to what questions these ethical and religious "answers" are directed. History, the New Testament, and the Reformation furnish "answers," material, words, propositions whose content is analyzed. But to what questions this historical material furnishes answers is not examined in the analysis of motifs. It is presupposed that the categorical and fundamental questions have already been defined in another discipline.

Nygren states specifically: "Motif research operates on the boundary between philosophy and history. It contains both a philosophical and an historical problem. In regard to its starting point it belongs with the presuppositional, philosophical analysis and the principle of categories there developed. It is in the confrontation of these categories, established by the presuppositional, philosophical analysis, with the concrete historical material that it becomes necessary to inquire about fundamental motifs. Motif research does not approach the historical material with indifferent kinds of questions, and consequently not everything or anything can be seized upon and regarded as a fundamental motif. It seeks answers to very definite questions; viz., the fundamental questions of categorical nature. Consequently only that which is appropriate as an answer to

15

such a categorical question can be regarded as a fundamental motif." [13]

If the historical material gives an oblique answer to the philosophically defined question, it would show only that the question was not completely formal. Formality means void of content; a condition which implies that the question does not clash with anything in the concrete material. All the historical material flows without friction into the form, provided that form is empty. The critical, philosophical task is to clarify the fundamental questions until they become completely formal.[14] Motif research will then attain to the highest possible exactness since in its analysis of the historical material it is not distracted by a philosophy of any particular attitude to life. It is the various conceptions of and attitudes to life which impart a content to the questions and destroy their pure formalism. This also precludes an objective observation of the fundamental motifs, which is exactly the task of theology.

The Christian message of God as forgiving Agape is, according to Nygren, an answer to a question posed by philosophy, a formal question devoid of content. *"The question is philosophically posed, the answer must be derived from the given historical reality."* Against this proposition we can on good historical grounds advance the following thesis: the Christian message of God as forgiving Agape is in reality an answer to a pregnant question, viz., the question of guilt. This message is meaningless unless the man who hears it is standing under

[13] *Filosofi och motivforskning, op. cit.,* p. 44 ff.
[14] When Nygren states in *Agape and Eros, op. cit.,* p. 42, that the fundamental motif is an answer to a fundamental question of categorical nature, he affirms the connection between philosophy and motif research. When he later in this context asserts that the fundamental questions themselves have changed, it must mean that they have not previously been completely formal.

the claim of God even before he hears the gospel. There is a continual danger that in Nygren's theology the center of the Christian faith, the gospel, becomes erroneously interpreted, since the gospel is divorced from the question of guilt and tied to a formal, philosophical question. Just this formality is the chief hindrance to a correct appraisal of the material. This hindrance cannot be removed *within* Nygren's theology. It is his very method of approach to the historical material that makes a correct interpretation of it impossible.

This critical observation can be based solely on his treatment of the fundamental religious question and his definition of the task of scientific dogmatics. But the observation is corroborated and the criticism sustained when we see clearly how he deals with the fundamental question of ethics and how he defines the objective of a scientific theological ethics. Here, too, the Christian message of Agape, in the sense of love to neighbor, constitutes the Christian answer to a formal, philosophical question: a concrete content poured into an empty categorical form: fellowship. This historical content is secondary in relation to the gospel and faith in the gospel. It follows from faith, flows out of the gospel already received. This whole theological ethics is a description of "the new man." Theological ethics has nothing to say about a man who has not heard the gospel, or who just now hears it. This silence is not accidental so that it could be corrected. The types of ethos are historically given, just as the religions are the historically existing religions described in history of religion.

Over against Christianity with its ethos stands the ethos of Platonism, Judaism, etc. The content or the answers lie in the historical sources. Theology must either describe Christianity with the gospel of God's Agape as the starting point and an ethos based on the gospel, or else it must describe another faith and type of ethos found in certain other historical sources. With this program theology can never produce a description of man determined by God's claim and by his own unbelief at the very time that he hears the gospel. It cannot be denied that such a description is a very difficult task for scientific theology. But if the gospel is even to be *described* as gospel, it must answer to the question of guilt, and not descend into an ethically void situation; a situation which is to be filled with ethical content from the ethos which is derived from the gospel.

It is again "formality" that is the chief hindrance to a correct presentation. Agape is a fundamental motif which answers a formal question both when it appears in the center of a faith (religious) and as center in an ethos (ethical). The content of the question which the message of God's Agape really answers, namely, the question of guilt, cannot be delineated in either the one or the other contexts as long as we adhere to the first part of Nygren's program. If the description were concerned with this question, the formality would be eliminated. Nor is this question raised in the second part of his program, the dogmatics and theological ethics, because here he simply describes a pregnant, fundamental motif, while he definitely declares that this motif is an answer to the fundamental questions of categorical nature which theology itself does not define. They are defined already when theology begins its work. This whole program is such that certain definite questions are in principle excluded. If it becomes apparent that the content of scripture cannot be presented while those questions are ignored, then it means that the method of approach in Nygren's theology clashes with the content of scripture. We do not here take into consideration that the question of truth is in principle excluded from theology. That has often been pointed out, and properly so. But from our point of view it is more significant that it becomes impossible to show clearly that the message of God's Agape really gives an answer to the question of guilt.

This surprising preliminary result of our investigation implies that the purely formal character of the question directed to the New Testament prevents a correct conception of the New Testament text. The formality, i.e., the lack of all content, ought to make the question really open so that the material would completely determine the answer. Instead we find that this formality disturbs the comprehension of the material. This must mean that the formalism itself, the critical approach, the striving after a formal, critical philosophy of this kind contains in reality a concrete, pregnant conception of life which clashes with the concrete, pregnant faith which is found in the New Testament. What is said in the New Testament is based on the presupposition that God has done a great deal in reference to mankind *before* he sent Jesus Christ into the world. It is impossible to come to this historical material with a question that is not determined by the biblical faith, and then select from this material only this one part, the New Testament, in order to force an answer from these sources to a categorical and fundamental question which is unrelated to those sources.

The gospel is a part, the most important part, in a history of salvation in which creation, the election of Israel, the covenants, etc., also belong. If it is separated from this context, it is no longer a "gospel," nor a witness to that Agape of which the New Testament speaks. The gospel acquires its meaning through its connections forward and backward, to creation and to the consummation. The gospel itself presupposes that every man to whom it comes stands subjected to the conditions of God's acts even before he hears it, and asks his questions in view of this condition: the questions of guilt and servitude. Since the message of God as Agape is primarily a message of God as the forgiver, this whole "ancient" relationship between God and man is a part of this message. Even the concept of "forgiveness" includes a very definite relationship between him who forgives and the one who receives forgiveness—a relationship which is altered in and through the act of forgiveness. The question to which the word of forgiveness is an answer is a question with a very definite content, the content of guilt. He who empties the question of this content represents a different view of life, filled with a definite and different content.

In this connection we must pay attention to a feature in Nygren's thinking already referred to: the fact that he adds certain productive forms of culture to a positivistically conceived science. Man stands observing theoretically without being subjected to any commandments or having any form of religion. He accepts the scientific propositions, but beyond them he sees nothing that is certain, only questions. In history, apart from himself, he observes historically existing religions. One "religion" mentioned sometimes in the New Testament is the worship of Mammon, but this religion is in reality not "historically given." [15] The New Testament conception is that Mammon can appear as anti-God always and everywhere. The assumption that religion is an historically given religion which has been produced in certain sources is foreign to the New Testament, but it is a self-evident presupposition in Nygren's philosophy of religion. Other "answers," other "contents," are not taken into consideration.

[15] Matt. 6:24. See also Col. 3:5; Phil. 3:19; Rom. 16:18. Mammon is probably not the name of a god, as the older exegesis assumed. Cf. J. B. Lightfoot, *Saint Paul's Epistles to the Colossians and to Philemon*, (London, 1879), p. 212.

The New Testament also maintains that human actions are under subjection even where the gospel is not heard; but this subjection is not to a different, historically given type of ethos, but a subjection under the law. Nygren assumes that man is void of "ethical ideals" until he chooses one historically given, but this assumption is foreign to the New Testament. The New Testament speaks rather of man's subjection and reckons with man's guilt before he makes his choice, yes, even before he hears the gospel. God is the God of creation and of the law, who for a long time and in various ways has dealt with mankind, but who now in the gospel proclaimed in the New Testament performs a new act in reference to them. The whole conception of this continuous subjection on the basis of earlier acts of God is destroyed when Nygren removes the New Testament material from this context and makes it answer questions which bear the imprint of modern conceptions of life and modern anthropology.

It is unquestionably difficult to present the biblical material in a scientific analysis. Scientific procedure is a particular human function which cannot be altered by dictates of the Christian faith. It is characteristic of its procedure that the scientist in asking his questions disengages himself from the object of his search. Such questions are foreign to the biblical writings. We have learned to use this procedure in a relatively recent European period which has been characterized by indifference to the content of scripture. It is naive to assume that the relationship between scientific study and the Bible should be free from difficulties. The only reasonable assumption is that the relationship is problematic. Whether it is possible to define the task of a scientifically working theology is something which we have to find out after many different attempts have been made. But it is certain that Nygren's attempt to define the task and the method of theology is not tenable.[16] The analyses which are essential to the understanding of the biblical material are in principle excluded by the very method of approach which Nygren proposes, namely, the combination of philosophy and motif research.

[16] It should be noted that what we criticize here is Nygren's methodological works. In his concrete historical research which resulted in *Agape and Eros* he has presented a great deal of material which had been neglected by theology and has placed it in a new context. At certain points we could raise the question whether these results do not constitute a critique and revision of his program. In the following chapter on motif research we shall have the opportunity to analyze Nygren's presentation of Marcion and Irenaeus. This presentation is very significant.

CHAPTER TWO

Antithesis: Gott-Mensch in Barth

It is characteristic of Karl Barth's thinking that God and man are understood as two different kinds of being. This ontology has left its stamp on his whole literary production. The changes which have taken place within his theology in the course of time are changes within this original framework. They may appear very large in the opinion of those who regard the antithesis, *Gott-Mensch*, as self-evident. But if we look at Barth's system from the outside—and thus we must look at it if we approach him from the point of view of the Bible or the Reformation—it is just this framework itself, this antithesis between divine and human existence, which is the most interesting part of his dogmatics. From this point of view the difference between earlier and later parts of Barth's theological production appears insignificant.

In general Barth does not describe the relationship between God and man as an antithesis in the sense of hostility. Normally the divine is described as being higher than and superior to the human. Superiority and inferiority become the distinctive marks of the two parties in the relationship. But there may also be found statements which imply that God is engaged in a real warfare with man. References to this are not limited to his commentary on Romans and other earlier writings. In *Offenbarung, Kirche, Theologie*, (1934), he describes revelation in the following manner: On the field of battle it has happened that the enemy with superior forces has taken the initiative and begun the attack. The troops in the front line send a courier message concerning the attack to the reserves in the rear. The enemy is God, the troops in the front line are the prophets and apostles who call to the church in the second line of defense. This report, this call, to those in the rear who have not yet been attacked, is scripture, the word of the prophets and the apostles to us, the church. "We do not understand either these men or this book unless we understand it in this way." [1] But before the troops in the front line call, i.e., before scripture is produced, God has already begun the attack on those in the front line. This initial action is the revelation, "God's revelation of himself to men . . . and he who does not understand it in this way does not know what he says when he uses the word revelation." [2] Further on it is asserted that revelation itself indicates the difference between God and man, and at the same time that the revelation discloses God's will to fellowship with men, and therefore also the relationship between God and man.[3]

This particular passage is very interesting since here the gospel of the Bible is really understood as a courier message, a kerygma. But in that case this kerygma is a call to men who are slaves, and who are now being told that they have been liberated by God's own intervention "on the field of battle," to use Barth's own expression. Barth is not and never has been accustomed to describe salvation from "such a military point of view." But he has noticed nevertheless certain biblical points of connection with the perspective of struggle and victory, and he knows how essential this perspective is for the Eastern

[1] K. Barth, *Offenbarung, Kirche, Theologie*, (*Theol. Exist. heute* 9) (1934), p. 16.
[2] *Ibid.*
[3] *Ibid.*, pp. 18-20.

churches, who have simply retained it from the early church, and also for Luther. But even though he sometimes employs this aspect of warfare, as for example in the article just referred to, he is compelled to distort the biblical word to some extent. On "the field of battle," as Barth describes it, there can be not more than two parties—God and Man. There is in Barth's theology no active power of sin, no tyrannical, demonic power that subjects man to slavery and which God destroys in his work of redemption. There is no devil in Barth's theology. This is a constant feature in his theological production.

The reason for this situation is that there was no evil power in the liberal theology against which Barth continually reacts. He has not penetrated beneath the liberal period in order to find in more profound eras the real help that he needs for the difficult task of interpreting scripture. At the very start he has simply turned liberal theology upside down; he has moved the accent within liberal theology from "man" to "God," but he has not been able to break up the structure of the problem. In Schleiermacher, says Barth, man was the central object of theological thinking.[4] God was something secondary in the system. God came in for consideration because man, the chief character, possessed religion, piety. Over against this caricature of Christian theology Barth wants to make God the center. He accomplishes this change by refusing to start either with religion or piety, and instead begins with the Word directed to man, which is God's address to man, and which never can become man's possession or a quality in himself.[5] It is clear that Barth remains within the framework

[4] K. Barth, *Die protestantische Theologie im 19 Jahrhundert* (Zürich, 1947), p. 410.

[5] This general attitude characterizes both the "Christian" dogmatics from the 1920 decade and the dogmatics of "the church" from the beginning of the 1930 decade. *Die christliche Dogmatik* I (1927) p. 450 ff., and

of Schleiermacher's theology, but rearranges freely within this frame so that God's freedom and superiority become clearly expressed. He himself is perfectly assured that his attempt is congruent with the theology of the reformers. The special anchorage which the Reformation had in the problem of penance, and consequently also in the problem of guilt and righteousness before God, Barth is not able to see very clearly. He assumes that his own problems are exactly those of the sixteenth century.[6]

If the fundamental question concerns guilt and righteousness,

Die kirchliche Dogmatik I:2 (1938), pp. 967-71. In and by itself it would be possible to express clearly a biblical content through these formulations. But when we discover the fundamental ontology, it becomes clear how far removed Barth really is from the questions dealt with in the Bible.

[6] Cf. K. Barth, *Weihnacht* (1934), p. 49, where Barth explains the well-known expression of Luther in one of his Christmas hymns: . . . *gibt der Welt ein neuen Schein*. He says: "Luther never claimed that he could find this *neuen Schein* in his heart or life, or in general in any human circumstances or conditions ('works' as they were usually called then)." When Luther says "works" or "achievements," we cannot without further ado substitute "human circumstances and conditions," since these works are what the law demands and constitute therefore civil or earthly righteousness. But the gospel, on the other hand, bestows a righteousness which does not consist in our works but in the forgiveness of sins. The main question with Luther is the question of righteousness. But with Barth the main question is whether we have knowledge of God, or whether in ourselves we lack such knowledge and must receive it from the outside. These are two entirely different questions. Luther holds that natural law compels us to do works; there is no encroachment on the gospel which deals with an entirely different righteousness. The gospel retains its unique position. Barth cannot bear to hear about a natural law, because in that case the will of God would be known independently of the incarnation, and the revelation in Christ would only complement something natural, i.e., something human. The positions of Barth and Luther are incompatible and cannot at all be reconciled. It is remarkable that Barth, who otherwise possesses keen insight, cannot see this, but rather continually imagines that he preserves the intentions of Luther. Lately, however, he seems to have become aware of how great the gulf is between him and Luther. All friends of historical truth would welcome a more general recognition of this fact both by Barth and by the Barthians.

or slavery and freedom, it is irrelevant to come with a word of revelation in which God's superiority over man is something essential. But the gospel, a message of forgiveness and victory, would be a very suitable answer to the fundamental question. It is the uniqueness of the Reformation, especially the Lutheran Reformation, that it has developed a fundamental question which is congruent with the biblical material. The slavery under the law in ancient Israel had in a sense returned under the guise of the medieval practice of penance. The real content of the New Testament, the gospel, found again its ancient foe, righteousness by the law, and was able again to manifest its power in the great crisis of the sixteenth century.

But Barth's question is the question of the twentieth century. During the nineteenth century civilization in general had lost interest in the idea of a righteousness before God and at the same time also the consciousness of guilt. The center of religion was faith in man and his inner life. God was transformed into a projection of human experiences and events. We could even say that man's superiority over God was characteristic of that era. There was no enslaving, evil power over man, nothing from which he needed to be set free. It is clear that the criticism of such an era can be carried through theologically, as Barth does, by emphasizing God's superiority over man. But it is just as clear that by doing so no contact is made with what is central in the Bible and in the Reformation. One only reacts, expresses the opposite, turns something upside down. Such a procedure always implies that one remains within the frame of reference of one's opponent.

Whoever begins his theological remodeling as Barth did in his commentary on Romans sooner or later becomes aware that he has made a mistake. In Barth's later writings we can see plainly that he tries to correct his mistake and that he endeavors more than ever to indicate that God's encounter with man implies that God acknowledges and rescues him.[7] But when Barth thus corrects himself, it never implies that he begins a new building. The foundation was laid in the earlier works, and that is never changed. This indicates that he cannot correct himself. The fundamental mistake in the system cannot be removed within the old structure. The removal of the fundamental mistake would mean the destruction of his theology. It is his own methodological approach to the historical material that prevents a correct understanding of it. In the following discussion we intend to explain this critical thesis at certain points which are signficant in reference to his anthropology. The examples cited are selected at random.

The self-evident frame of reference for Barth's whole theology is in general the following. God has a certain nature. Man has a certain nature. The latter has no knowledge of the former, unless the former reveals himself to the latter. But now God has revealed himself to man. This revelation occurred in Jesus Christ. "The word became flesh" (John 1:14). The incarnation becomes the center of theology and is understood as a revelation of God to man. The frame of reference consists of these three elements: (1) God as an unknown being until he reveals himself, and henceforth as known; (2) man without knowledge of God and directed to the place where God reveals himself; and finally (3) this concept of revelation. All three of these elements—God, man, revelation—are typically biblical elements. It must be emphasized, too, that the revelation is Christ, who is at the same time God and man. This simple framework appears entirely scriptural.

But it is exactly this framework which is questionable. "Revelation" stands in the place where "justification," or "for-

[7] See *Die kirchliche Dogmatik* IV:1 (1953), p. 94f. and 203f.

giveness of sins," i.e., the gospel in the essential meaning of that word, ought to stand. If "justification" stands in the center, it is assumed that man already knows something; yes, that God has already "revealed" himself through his work in creation (Rom. 1:20), although he has not disclosed his plan of salvation in this creation. Man is driven to do something, but his works do not give him life; he pursues righteousness, but he does not attain to it. He stands there, not without knowledge but "without excuse," consequently with guilt, just because already as man he has had to deal with God and therefore knows how he ought to live. The uniqueness of the gospel, therefore, is that it reveals a new righteousness, apart from the law, a righteousness from God through faith in Jesus Christ (Rom. 3:21 ff.). The law was given through Moses (John 1:17), and it works already in what the Gentiles do; and the word "do" is important in this connection.[8]

In Christ, however, a righteousness by grace is revealed which is not based on works which man performs (Titus 3:3-7). But this biblical line of thought cannot find a place within a frame of reference determined by these three elements: the being of God, the being of man, and revelation. The frame of reference must be constituted by three other elements: the works of God, the works of man, and justification. Within such a framework we may also use *"Seins"*-categories and talk about what God is and what man is, just as we may also use the term revelation to clarify what has

---

[8] Rom. 2:14. Passages like this cause great difficulty for Barthian exegesis, since they seem to take away the significance of the revelation in Christ. But Rom. 2:14 does not speak of *salvation*. Even if the works of the Gentiles were altogether good, they could not bring what the gospel gives: the salvation of man in Christ "apart from works." The difficulty appears only after the general concept of "revelation" has been put in the center and the question about "righteousness" and "justification" has been shunted aside. In the text itself there is no difficulty on this point.

taken place in Christ. But in that case what God is becomes evident through his dealings with the world, and what man is becomes apparent in his work, i.e., in his sin. His lack of knowledge of God does not become the chief concern. Consequently, what is essential in the revelation in Christ is the new act of God in him, a righteousness by grace, not a knowledge imparted to man concerning an otherwise unknown God.[9]

If we are to discover the critical point in Barth's theology, we must concentrate our attention on the essential structure, the framework itself. If we simply note what Barth says within this framework, we miss that which is typical in his theology. Then the word about Christ dominates the whole. But the question must be asked: Why must this biblical word be forced into this frame? Does it not lose its content and significance when forced into this frame?

We must first point out clearly that this framework is never abandoned. We might assume, of course, that the limitations might be transcended. Barth's conception that God became man could be given such a content that the frame would break. God, one being, became man, the other being. But this does not happen in Barth's presentation of the incarnation.

"God cannot cease to be God." [10] The incarnation means that God appropriates to himself human existence. The word of God is present with us in Christ in such a way that "he takes to himself the human existence, which is his creation, and makes it his own existence (Sein)." [11] The statement,

---

[9] Barth definitely rejects the idea that justification should stand in the center, and regards it as a confessional Lutheran characteristic that justification has this place in Lutheran theology. See Die kirchliche Dogmatik IV:1, pp. 581-89.

[10] Die kirchliche Dogmatik I:2, p. 175.   [11] Ibid., p. 176.

"the word became flesh," ought to be rendered "the word assumed flesh." We find a line of thought in Barth which strongly emphasizes that the gulf between the divine and the human remains unbridged even in the incarnation. This is the idea, presented especially in *Die kirchliche Dogmatik* III:2 (1948), that the humanity of Jesus Christ mirrors the divine in Jesus Christ.[12] The idea of a mirror or a reflection occurs frequently in Barth's writings, and it means everywhere the same: a distance between two spheres; and, in addition, a reflection of the relatively higher sphere in the lower. This conception dominates Barth's doctrine of the sacraments, and is likewise the key to his political ethics.[13] The human may contain something that points to or "reminds" of the divine. The idea of reflection appears also in Christology and extends, therefore, to that which the Word of God assumed in the incarnation, i.e., the humanity of Jesus Christ. The frame—God, man, revelation—is never broken. The chief significance of the incarnation continues to be: "God" (a being of whom "man" has no knowledge) reveals himself to "man" (so that "man" receives knowledge of "God" from Christ.)

We must also take note of this unqualified conception of "revelation." It would be possible to maintain that "revelation" in Barth is the antithesis to "natural knowledge of God," the antithesis to the thesis that man of himself, by nature, does not know anything about God. This general term—revelation—dominates Barth's system because it is useful in connection with this antithesis. The dominant position of this term makes it possible to retain the gulf between the two kinds of nature (*Sein*). If, however, we assume that God is what he *does*, and

[12] *Op. cit.*, III:2, pp. 247 ff., 258, 161, 267 ff., etc.
[13] K. Barth, *Die christliche Lehre von der Taufe (Theol. Studien 14)* (1943), p. 7 f. and p. 17 f. Tr. *The Teaching of the Church Regarding Baptism,* Ernest A. Payne (London, 1948).

if his activity consists in saving, giving and justifying, then we can easily see how this divine activity reaches its highest intensity in an incarnation characterized by humiliation.

When the Incarnate gave up his life on the cross, then occurred the action which is the supreme, divine event: the act of self-giving love. The divine was not diminished, it was raised to the highest degree in this impoverishment. When this event stands in the center, the resurrection does not appear as a return from the lowliness and weakness of the purely human to the divine nature. Rather, the resurrection is the transition to the universal, divine outpouring of love in the preaching of the gospel to the ends of the earth; that is, God's continual descent with the gospel of the righteousness by grace into the depths of guilt from man to man until the end of the world. What is "revealed" in the gospel is, therefore, salvation in contrast to guilt and bondage. To bestow such righteousness and freedom is a divine act. But this act of God takes place in the humiliation of Christ; in the fact that Christ does not grasp after equality with God, but empties himself and is found in human form. From the point of view of activity God appears most clearly in that which, from the point of view of Being, seems most human, the destitution of the cross. But then it becomes impossible to draw the line between divine and human nature as Barth does. Here the unqualified concept of revelation, i.e., that the higher being makes himself known to the lower, is not the dominant concept. Man's predicament is not that he lacks knowledge, but that he is guilty. He is guilty because he knew what he ought to do, but he pursued his own works against God.

The Barthian idea, referred to above, that the human "points to" or "mirrors" the divine becomes clearer if we note carefully what possibilities Barth excludes and rejects. In the first place, he denies that God is ever the subject in any human activity.[14] God does not enter the human in such a way that he himself does anything on earth in human form. Typical in this respect is the main outline of his angelology as he develops this in *Die kirchliche Dogmatik* III:3 (1950). This book has not aroused much interest, perhaps because of the peculiar subject matter, the life of the angels; but it is one of the writings in which Barth's conception of the relationship between God and man appears most clearly. Man can never meet God in his deity. To be sure, man standing in the cosmos may bear witness to God. But this is something which must be given to man from above, for in himself he is from below. The witness is given to men in that God meets man in the cosmos through these mediators, the angels, the chief witnesses. "It happens first in heaven and then on earth that God is praised by the creature, that God finds his creaturely counterparts and witnesses." [15] God is and remains in heaven. How he can work on earth is a problem for Barth. Therefore the angels are interposed between God and man. But when this is done, the main point is not that they perform work which is God's work on earth through them, but that they are the first who "bear witness," "reflect," or who are God's "counterparts" and "mirror."

This fact, that God is not conceived of as working *in* anything human, using the human as an instrument or means for his own divine acts on earth, this negative relationship, is of tremendous importance in Barth's theology. As a consequence Barth is unable to conceive of the law as an act of God by

---

[14] See *Die kirchliche Dogmatik* III:4, 1951, p. 596 ff. "Gottes Tun geschieht nie 'in und unter,' sondern freilich mit, aber immer über und gegenüber dem menschlichen Tun."

[15] *Die kirchliche Dogmatik* III:3, p. 540. Cf. pp. 584; 581-83; 541.

which God incites human activity. In that case it would be possible to interpret those passages in the New Testament which assume that good works may be done outside of the sphere of the preaching of the gospel as dealing with God's guidance and rule over the world through the law (Rom. 13:1-10, for example.)[16] God's activity would then be the dominant point of view.

There would then be no contradiction in the idea that God through Christ establishes a kingdom other than the kingdoms of this world. But on the basis of such a universal rule of God in and through the law the existence of guilt and its connection with human life would be understood. It would then also be easily understood that when the gospel comes, it meets men who are guilty. Barth, on the contrary, as soon as he hears the word "law," presupposes something entirely different. The law is knowledge on the part of man within the relationship *Gott-Mensch*. If the law were given where the gospel is not yet given, it would imply that man, as he encounters the gospel, already through "the law" has a partial knowledge of God and his will, and thus the Word loses its position as lord over man.[17] It is strange that we must make this statement, but it is necessary: in Barth's theology man is the obvious center. The question about man's knowledge is the axis around which the whole subject matter moves. On the basis of this central point it is natural—if the lordship of God rather than

[16] In that case the necessity for a christological interpretation of Romans 13 disappears. The need for such an interpretation has arisen under the influence of Barthian theology. The obvious meaning of the text as it stands and as it has been understood through the centuries is incompatible with this theology. Exegesis must then finally be employed to relieve the situation.

[17] *Die kirchliche Dogmatik* II:1, 1940, p. 407. Here faith is inserted as the bearer of the witness concerning God's judgment, and from this Barth draws the conclusion that the gospel precedes the law.

that of man is to be emphasized—to maintain that there is only one revealed word from which the law is derived, and thus propose the order: gospel and law.[18]

That man's knowledge and insight rather than God's activity are the center is clearly evident from what Barth says about the law. God's will is, to be sure, supreme in everything that happens. But, he maintains, God's will is not revealed in everything that happens; "namely so revealed that our recognition of it could claim to be something more than or different from our own theories or interpretations." [19] Only when grace is revealed, the whole will of God is revealed. The whole of God's will is revealed first in the word of Christ, the gospel. From this Barth draws the conclusion that the gospel is primary and the law is contained in the gospel. This conclusion is valid only if "revelation" is the leading point of view, but Barth has never demonstrated that this is the case. Rather, he starts with this thesis as something axiomatic and self-evident.

When the idea of revelation becomes the governing point of view, man's realization of the revelation becomes in fact the dominant point of view. But if God's activity is permitted to occupy the center, there is every reason to speak of God's work in creation even before the gospel. God's activity in the salvation of humanity comprises a long series of acts which God has done, does, and will do. We can start at any one point and proceed backward and forward. But anyone who poses the question, "Where is all this revealed to us?" places man's knowledge in the foreground; in a certain sense he anticipates the clarity of eschatological seeing. For in this sense God's activity never becomes "revealed" in this world, not

[18] K. Barth, *Evangelium und Gesetz (Theol. Exist. heute 32)* (1935), pp. 9-12. It is important for Barth to show how the law is *revealed.*
[19] *Ibid.,* p. 9.

35

even to faith. That can happen only in the resurrection from the dead and the last judgment when God's series of acts really are finished.

The concept of counterpart (*Entsprechung*) always means the same for Barth: a correspondence, a reflection through which something divine is mirrored. From our point of view the most interesting use of this term counterpart is found in *Die kirchliche Dogmatik* III:3, where he designates evil as such a counterpart, viz., a counterpart to the divine non-will (*Nichtwollen*). Consequently Barth often uses non-being (*das Nichtige*) to designate evil. "Non-being is that which God does not will. It exists simply as being that which God does not will. But just on that account it exists, because not only God's will but also his non-will is power and cannot be without a real counterpart. The real counterpart to the divine non-will is non-being." [20]

We must compare such statements with what he says in *Die kirchliche Dogmatik* III:1 (1945) in his exegesis of the story of creation. When God began creating, this positive choice implied that there was something which he did not do, something which he "despised and passed by," a possibility which he did not will. This possibility which God despised and passed by is chaos, something which in principle is passed by and no longer exists.[21] But since man is non-divine, he can act as if what God has rejected really is something. This human act, sin in its real sense, is an ontological mistake. But the mistake can be made; and when it is made, it becomes at the same time rebellion and disobedience.

In *Die kirchliche Dogmatik* III:3, Barth develops with great clarity how this non-being (*das Nichtige*), on the one hand,

[20] *Op. cit.*, III:3, p. 406.
[21] *Op. cit.*, III:1, p. 119 f.

lacks objective existence, and, on the other hand, how it becomes a power "in our blind eyes." Because we falsely regard it as being something, it actually becomes by our perverted faith a power which determines our attitude and our actions. Only when God becomes revealed in Christ does non-being also stand revealed as nothing, having no objective existence. "From the point of view of Jesus Christ it cannot be said about non-being that it still has any objective existence, or that it remains except before our still veiled eyes, or that it is still to be feared. . . ." [22] In this connection it becomes clear that the fundamental sin is false thinking and that, on the contrary, faith becomes correct thinking. The verb *denken* prevails in the description.

To this conception the idea of "revelation" is perfectly analogous. The power which non-being has over us is an illusion; but it is a dangerous illusion with a real power because we do not know the essential reality. We are continuously deceived. "Non-being can have value or attain validity only insofar as universal revelation has not yet been finished, as the whole creation still waits for it and looks forward to it." [23] Here a part of the realization is transferred to the eschatological future when the complete "revelation" will be given and no one will any more think falsely. But the meaning which "revelation" has here is the meaning which Barth constantly gives to it. The essential point is that evil is not a power opposed to God which God in a new act defeats on the last day. There are no new acts or events to be expected.[24] Every-

[22] *Op. cit.*, III:3, p. 419.

[23] *Ibid.*, p. 424.

[24] "It is not proper to think of non-being as if the real redemption or freedom from it were a matter of some future time or an expected event." (*Ibid.*, p. 420). Barth likens evil to a hornet without a sting. The movement of the hornet may inspire fear in a person who does not know

thing has already taken place. What we lack is insight. There is no evil power standing side by side with the kingdom of God, even though it may appear so to our blinded eyes. Revelation tells us that this is an illusion.

It is evident that the acts of God are removed from the picture when we concentrate our attention on being (*Sein*) and appearance (*Schein*). There can be no doubt but that Barth on this point departs from the explicit statements of scripture. But it does not seem to be generally recognized how essential and theologically destructive this departure is. Barth criticizes somewhat humorously the New Testament statements dealing with the fall of the angels (Jude 6 and II Pet. 2:4), whereby created beings, i.e., beings whom God willed, became evil and opposed to God. These statements naturally contradict Barth's ideas about non-being (*das Nichtige*), and he cannot tolerate them, even though they are found in scripture. "A real, honest-to-goodness angel does not do anything like that . . . "[25]

The bantering style in which he presents his argument indicates that he regards it as belonging to the periphery of the Bible, where he may add and subtract as he likes without thereby affecting the central elements of the Bible. But when the opposition to God loses its reality, then also God's character as the living and active God becomes obscured and his coming is interpreted as "revelation" in a sense foreign to the New Testament. It becomes an unveiling of the divine nature and an exposé of the empty illusion. In this way the question of man's knowledge becomes the central problem. A man

that the sting has been removed. But such a person is mistaken. The power of the hornet depends entirely on this mistake, not on anything that the hornet possesses. Man needs only to be told how it really is.

[25] *Ibid.*, p. 623. "And furthermore we must say that no demon has ever really been in heaven. They just act as if they came directly from there."

38

who has not heard the revealed word lacks knowledge. A man who hears the revealed word receives knowledge.

In 1932 Barth began his dogmatics anew and in so doing openly rejected his existential-philosophical point of departure. At the same time he began his attack on natural theology. Since that time his concentration on the question of man's knowledge and insight has resulted in a negative bias in his anthropology. Man lacks knowledge of God, but he receives this knowledge through the revelation in Christ. The positive anthropology which he developed during the second half of the 1940-49 decade produced no change in this respect. It is the very subtlety of this positive anthropology that it does not imply a return to the position held before the debate with Emil Brunner, and that the question about man's knowledge is not affected. The negative formulation of the question of knowledge remains.

When we deal with the hermeneutical presuppositions in the next chapter, we will have occasion to point out what this means in regard to the positive definition of such concepts as "the Word of God" and "revelation." Just now we are interested chiefly in the negative definition in the doctrine of man. This appears most clearly in his denial of any natural knowledge of God. But before we try to indicate the significance of this denial, it is advisable to say something about the difference between the "Christian Dogmatics" of 1927 and the "Church Dogmatics" from 1932 onward. We must note carefully how the existential-philosophical element is removed. This is really a question of simple subtraction. In consequence it becomes clearer that negation is really the characteristic mark of Barth.

In 1927 Barth began with a phenomenological starting point. He establishes that preaching is now going on, and he declares that the task of dogmatics is to examine this preaching and determine whether it is true or not.[26] He then brings the listener into the picture, and this means that he himself participates. We participate "existentially." "If in the future we would occasionally make use of phenomenological thinking, it can be done in no other way than that definitely and openly we subordinate it to existential thinking." [27] This subordination of the Word under existential formulations appears very clearly in this first work on dogmatics. Existential thinking is regarded as a given and known entity, and the proclaimed Word is problematic. The former holds the key to the latter. "The Word of God is a concept that is accessible only to existential thinking." [28] To be sure, Barth's subordination is not as radical as Bultmann's was at that time and later. But he pursued the conjunction between dogmatic interpretation of "the Word of God" and existential-philosophical anthropology so far that, when a few years later he takes a more critical attitude toward Heidegger and existentialism, he concludes that he cannot continue with volume two of a dogmatics so conceived. Instead he starts over again with *Die kirchliche Dogmatik*. Some of the subjects discussed previously are repeated in the new work. But here this kind of anthropology has been removed and openly denied.[29]

When the Word of God is imprisoned in an anthropology that is constructed independently of the word of scripture,

[26] *Die christliche Dogmatik* I, p. 1 ff.

[27] *Ibid.*, p. 49.

[28] *Ibid.*, p. 111.

[29] *Die kirchliche Dogmatik* I:1, p. 166. "This decision is possible only as an answer to the Word of God spoken to me. It is not a special case among the possibilities of human decisions in general. It cannot be understood within the framework of a general anthropology. Even the most radical crisis in which man in general understands himself anthropologically has nothing to do with this crisis."

God loses his freedom. Now Barth is of the opinion that by his earlier concern with "existentialism" he had tied down dogmatics to a principle which renders the sovereignty of God impossible. "But from this point of view it becomes clear how precarious it is to incorporate the doctrine of the Word of God within the framework of an anthropology. The sovereignty of the divine purpose for man can then be emphasized only as an afterthought, although it is really denied by this approach." [30] Man is, of course, concerned in the word which God speaks, since God freely elects to speak with him, but this is not an essential necessity, "which I astonishingly enough maintained in the first edition." [31]

Barth's decisive objection to Bultmann is already given here in his criticism of the existential approach, this "no" to any suggestion of using Heidegger's philosophy. His negative attitude to Bultmann is to a large degree justified, and we will have occasion to discuss this pro and con later on. Here we are interested primarily in Barth himself. It should be noted that his argument results in a vacuum as far as anthropology is concerned. In this respect Barth differs from the other two theologians, Nygren and Bultmann, who both combine their theology with a concrete philosophy. In a certain sense the uniqueness of Barth lies in his pure assumption of a content taken from the biblical writings, viz., revelation. But for the positive definition of this biblical content it is important to note that the counterpart on man's side is something negative: man's lack of knowledge of God.

It is a common rule that if a man answers "no" he denies

[30] *Ibid.*, p. 145.
[31] *Ibid.*, p. 111, footnote. This formulation is very significant. The address is therefore not an essential part of a letter because that would reduce the writer's sovereignty. This is related to the fact that Barth removes the dualism of law and gospel.

something which the questioner in some form or another accepts. But some questions cannot be answered by either yes or no. Even "no" implies something positive; it involves an acceptance of the opponent's question. Such an affirmative "no" is Barth's *Nein* in the year 1934. Barth is essentially dependent upon natural theology. The fundamental problem of natural theology rests on the fact that the starting point is in man, and that the attempt is made to find an explanation of how man can have knowledge of God. Since the question concerns man as man without reference to where or when he lives, the source of this knowledge cannot be Christ; it must instead be nature or creation in one form or another. Barth rejects this natural theology. He says *Nein* to it. But now the revelation in Christ has to give an answer to the same question. "We cannot, however, refuse to consider the problem itself. If God can be known, it is necessary to inquire in how far he is perceptible by man." [32] This implies that man and the content of scripture are placed in such a relationship that the content of scripture provides man with a knowledge of God which he otherwise lacks. The knowledge of God which man lacks he receives from scripture, i.e., from Christ. This is the simplest formula in which Barth's theology can be expressed. And about this formula we must say that it is entirely unbiblical. There is no possibility of interpreting the biblical writings correctly from this point of view.

Placing the question of knowledge in the center is in itself a pregnant theological thesis, no matter whether it is solved by the help of natural theology or by the exclusive concept of revelation. A person who receives a check in the mail certainly gains some knowledge when he takes the check and reads it. But if this is the main point that before he read the check he

[32] *Die kirchliche Dogmatik* II:1 (1940) p. 142.

lacked a certain knowledge which now has been given to him, he has a false conception of at least three realities. He has a false conception of his own situation before the check came, as if the absence of knowledge was the important part. He has a false conception of the function of a check, as if its primary function was to convey knowledge. And he has a false picture of the sender, as if he who was previously unknown now had made himself known. That which disappears from our attention through the theological work of Barth in this generation is the living and active God of the Bible, this God who continually creates and gives.

Any thought that, for example, the law is a government, an activity of God whereby he compels men to do works, cannot be included in a frame defined according to the question of knowledge. Then the law becomes immediately changed into a source of knowledge, and the question must then be raised: Is the knowledge of the law clear and correct, or is there something lacking which must be supplied through the word of grace in Christ? If it is clear and correct, it is also an agency of salvation, and then it really contains the gospel.[33] If it is unclear and incomplete, then it becomes fully "revealed" later; and, in that case, this later word, the gospel, becomes the primary. But we might also understand the law as an instrument for God's rule over the world; and therefore perceive it as active where the demand of the neighbor reaches me, see how it results in deeds and works of men living together in community, and finally also see how it builds up guilt in the consciences of all these who act and work. The gospel of God's act in Christ would then primarily mean the establishment of a different kingdom than the kingdom of human

[33] See K. Barth, *Nein (Theol. Exist. heute 14)* (1934), pp. 19, 42 f., 52 f. Also *Evangelium und Gesetz, op. cit.,* pp. 1-15.

works; a new gift of the active God who takes away sin and confers a new righteousness and eternal life. It would be meaningless then to derive the law from the gospel, and vice versa; for both are works of God. Their inner unity lies exclusively in God. Any suggestion of such a point of view is foreign to Barth, and he denies it with utmost energy wherever he finds it, and he believes that he finds it in Luther. But he has never seen that it is already to be found in the Bible.

We have limited ourselves to the anthropological presuppositions in Barth's theology, and considered only one such presupposition of a very simple and elementary kind, viz., man's lack of knowledge of God. Someone might argue that this is not an anthropological statement at all, and that Barth's doctrine of the common humanity and *analogia relationis* (developed in *Die kirchliche Dogmatik* III:2) is of far greater interest. But the simple, negative statement of man's lack of knowledge of God contains a very important anthropological presupposition. It determines Barth's conception of scripture. The word in the biblical writings is always interpreted so that it fills a vacuum which man's lack of knowledge implies. This elementary, negative presupposition in anthropology becomes in itself a positive presupposition in hermeneutics. Whatever fills a vacuum receives its contours from the empty space it has to fill.

44

CHAPTER THREE

Bultmann's Anthropology

Rudolf Bultmann combines anthropology and hermeneutics so intimately that it is impossible to discuss the anthropological problem by itself. The text itself demands an existential, or, as he sometimes calls it, an anthropological interpretation. The rules of interpretation, therefore, are to some extent contained in the anthropology. In this chapter, when we discuss Bultmann's anthropological presuppositions, we have to deal also with his views of scripture to a greater extent than was necessary in the case of Nygren and Barth. As far as possible, however, we will reserve the treatment of Bultmann's interpretation of the kerygma of the New Testament for discussion in the second part where it belongs.

As a convenient starting point we may take Bultmann's assertion about the meaninglessness of talking about the resurrection of Jesus as an actual occurrence. Aside from the fact that such an event appears to us incredible, the narrative itself is meaningless. It does not tell us anything important, even if it were true that it actually happened.[1] Modern man cannot understand how he could attain to fulness of life, to his "authentic being," by being involved in such a resurrection. "He would be able to see God's action only in an event which affects the reality of his own spiritual life and transforms his personality. But in the case of such a miracle of nature as the resuscitation of a dead body, even apart from its incredibility in

[1] *Kerygma and Myth, op. cit.,* p. 6 ff. See also *Kerygma und Mythos,* ed. Hans Werner Bartsch (Hamburg, 1952), II, 188 f., 192 f.

general, he cannot understand how that can be an act of God, or how this can affect his own life." [2] This statement deals primarily with modern man. It is a description of the attitude and the feeling of modern man. But this statement is also a part of a thesis: we must demythologize. This is really the main argument in the case. Not even in the subsequent positive presentation of his thesis does he for one moment relax his hold on this spontaneous attitude of modern man. Instead he deliberately makes modern man the norm. From one point of view what can be brought forth out of the New Testament is decided by the norm of modern man's understanding of himself.

This is not an opportunistic assertion. The motive for attaching the kerygma to modern man and his understanding of existence lies much deeper. By its very nature the kerygma exists for man, for a hearer, who receives his true life from the kerygma. If we come to Sweden with the gospel and start proclaiming it in Greek, it is not mere expediency to change to Swedish after it becomes apparent that the Greek means nothing to the hearers. But the transition from Greek to Swedish undoubtedly implies that we forsake the original formulation and use words unknown to the apostles. Nevertheless, the transition serves the content of the kerygma. To retain the original form would mean a concealment of this content. The claim that the kerygma offers true life to the hearer is correctly apprehended by this hearer only at the moment when he realizes that he is lost in himself and that he is saved by the message that comes to him from outside of himself. This alternation between "lost" and "saved" presupposes a common factor in the understanding of existence both in the kerygma and of the hearer.

It is Bultmann's fundamental conviction that modern man

[2] *Kerygma and Myth, op. cit.,* p. 8.

knows that he is lost.[3] The kerygma of salvation is meaning-less to him unless it does strike at the ailment of man; i.e., unless authentic existence means the same for both the kerygma and the hearer. This does not imply that man already possesses what the New Testament offers. The opposite is true. He lacks just that which the New Testament offers. He receives the new life from the Word.[4] But this want, this lostness must confront or meet the giving, the redemption. This meeting can take place only if the kerygma meets man in an existential interpretation.

We must note, however, that such an existential interpretation brings out the essential meaning of the text. The text is factually misunderstood unless it is interpreted in this way. All nonexistential interpretations reach only the periphery of the text. To interpret existentially is to apply a sound scientific method to the interpretations of these ancient texts. It is characteristic that Bultmann can point to Hans Jonas' work on Gnosticism as a model of interpretation of mythical docu-ments.[5] A study of this large work is very helpful for those who would understand Bultmann. Jonas interprets Gnosticism as due to a change in the very experience of life and a drastic dislocation within man's understanding of what human exist-ence really is: an experience of the world as foreign to man,

[3] *Ibid.*, p. 29.

[4] Cf. Ian Henderson, *Myth in the New Testament* (Chicago, 1952), p. 29. Since Bultmann's starting point is that man already knows what authentic life is, but is not able to set himself free for this life, but is dependent for obtaining it on "an act of God" presented in the kerygma, he escapes the fruitless and onesided emphasis on "knowledge," *die Erkenntnis Gottes*, which characterizes Barth's view of scripture. The character of the Word as action, liberating and creative action, is ex-pressed very clearly in Bultmann's presentation.

[5] *Kerygma and Myth, op. cit.*, p. 16. Hans Jonas, *Gnosis und spätanti-ker Geist* I (1934) pp. 47-49, 66 f., 74 f., 87, 170 f. The author's depend-ence on Heidegger appears clearly on p. 107.

and a feeling of the homelessness of the ego in the world. Out of these experiences, which are primary and constitute the very content of Gnosticism, arise various conceptions in which man's fundamental experience is expressed in a way that was understood at the time: heavenly spheres are introduced between the world and God, a demiurge is suggested as the creator of the world, etc. Anyone who merely describes and classifies these objectified conceptions understands nothing of the meaning of these gnostic texts. The task must be to interpret these gnostic texts existentially; i.e., in order to expose the understanding of existence which underlies these individual, concrete, crudely massive conceptions.[6]

We can understand Bultmann by noticing how the existential interpretation appears when it is applied to gnostic material. But Bultmann's interpretation is nevertheless different. He proposes the task of interpreting the New Testament message so that it engages modern man in his own existence, not merely that he apprehends that understanding of existence which once upon a time was expressed in the objective conceptions of primitive Christianity. The New Testament word is a kerygma, and we interpret it in this character as kerygma only when it reaches into and stands in relation to the present. But in addition, and this is typical of Bultmann, the New Testament understanding of existence is not only one among many possibilities. The kerygma receives support from philosophy. The New Testament conceives of human existence in the same

[6] *Kerygma and Myth, op. cit.,* p. 16. "The meaning of these two types of mythology lies once more not in their imagery with its apparent objectivity but in the understanding of human existence which both are trying to express. In other words, they need to be interpreted existentially. A good example of such treatment is to be found in Hans Jonas' book on Gnosticism. Our task is to produce an existentialist interpretation of the dualistic mythology of the New Testament along similar lines."

way that modern philosophy does.[7] And yet there is something in the New Testament kerygma which the philosopher finds unacceptable. It is important to note carefully how Bultmann proceeds at this point.

Bultmann asks first whether "the Christian understanding of being" is the same as "man's natural understanding of his being." This would mean that the New Testament has discovered an insight which in principle is available to all men. Now, when philosophy (and especially Heidegger's philosophy) has disclosed the real quality of human existence, nothing more need be expected from the New Testament. Philosophy has replaced theology.[8] We now know that man is not "tangible" like things; that he does not have qualities, but rather "possibilities," which means that he lives in "the decision." He can lose himself and remain imprisoned in the past; or, he can open himself to the future by throwing away all security and thereby attain to his "authentic nature." This is what existentialism maintains, and this is, as far as Bultmann is concerned, scientific truth.[9] This is identical with what the New Testament suggests by "faith." This reaching out toward the future, a future seized in the decision made in the present, is what is meant and intended by the New Testament eschatology,

[7] *Ibid.*, p. 24. "Above all, Heidegger's existentialist analysis of the ontological structure of being would seem to be more than a secularized, philosophical version of the New Testament view of human life. . . . Is not that exactly the New Testament understanding of human life? Some critics have objected that I am borrowing Heidegger's categories and forcing them upon the New Testament. I am afraid that this only shows that they are blinding their eyes to the real problem, which is that the philosophers are saying the same thing as the New Testament and saying it quite independently."

[8] *Ibid.*, p. 23.

[9] *Ibid.*, pp. 22-23. Bultmann shares the naïveté which characterizes a theologian who has accepted a certain concrete philosophy. A certain *philosopher* is quoted, and then it is asserted that *philosophy* has explained, proved, shown, etc.

no matter how much it is filled with concrete and fantastic imagery.

Does this now imply that "the Christian understanding of being" is the same as "man's natural understanding of being"? Bultmann's answer is typical. Philosophy *knows* what genuine "historic existence" involves. In this respect it has nothing to learn from the New Testament. The difference is not one of knowledge or insight. But philosophy assumes that all man needs is to be told what his authentic nature is, then he will be able to realize it.[10] The New Testament, however, maintains that man's authentic being is not under man's control. Even if man knows what he ought to be, he cannot become or realize it. If man is to be set free, it must be by an act independent of himself, by "an act of God." Every impulse of man, even his knowledge, is the impulse of a lost man which cannot liberate him. What is given in the New Testament, therefore, is not directly a doctrine of man's authentic being (this would avail nothing), but it is a message of an act in regard to man, "the proclamation of an act of redemption which was wrought in Christ." [11]

Bultmann is engaged in demythologizing, i.e., in interpreting concrete notions in such a way that they appear as bearers of an understanding of existence. But is not the conception of "an act of God" mythology? Should it not be translated into a statement that deals only with human existence? Would not otherwise a mythological fragment be left uninterpreted? The decisive difficulty lies in the fact that the New Testament idea of "an act of God" expresses a fundamental doctrine of New Testament anthropology; viz., that man is a lost sinner. We would surrender this anthropological doctrine if we gave up

[10] *Ibid.*, p. 27.
[11] *Ibid.*, p. 27.

the idea of "an act from outside of man." The question must, according to Bultmann, be turned around. Is sin a mythological concept? If the concept of sin is not mythological, then it is proved, in a roundabout way, that the idea of "an act of God" is not a mythological remnant, but, in spite of its peculiar form, it is really a statement about human existence, an inescapable part of the New Testament understanding of existence. To abandon this would mean a change in the understanding of existence.

It is evident that Bultmann thinks that sin cannot be discovered by human observation. Since sin comprises all that man does, he cannot see it. "Man's radical self-assertion then blinds him to the fact of sin, and this is the clearest proof that he is a fallen being. Hence it is no good telling man that he is a sinner. He will only dismiss it as mythology. But it does not follow that he is right. Sin ceases to be mere mythology when the love of God meets man as a power which embraces and sustains him even in his fallen, self-assertive state. Such a love treats man as if he were other than he is. By so doing, love frees man from himself as he is."[12] It is also evident that, according to Bultmann, sin ceases to be mythological when man encounters the love of God in *die Tat Gottes*, and when he thereby becomes "free from himself." But finally it is evident that Bultmann, even after he has finished his presentation, remains uncertain about his argument. Its circular character is evidently quite obvious to him. "Are there still any surviving traces of mythology? There certainly are for those who regard all language about an act of God or of a decisive, eschatological event as mythological. But in that case such mythology is not mythology in the traditional sense."[13] Our

[12] *Ibid.*, p. 31.
[13] *Ibid.*, p. 43.

interest is not in determining whether Bultmann has proved his point or not, but exclusively in the way in which the argument is presented. From that point of view we have to examine his presentation very carefully.

On one point in his anthropology Bultmann maintains a thesis for which he finds no support in his philosophers, either Heidegger or Kamlah, viz., the doctrine of sin. Bultmann simply makes a leap into the kerygma. He takes up his position outside of spontaneous self-judgment and looks at man as he is when he has become liberated from himself. Seeing sin as a total power is possible only on the basis of the redemptive act of God. This universal judgment on the ego can be made only from a point outside of the ego, at a point where the deliverance has taken place, a point which is attained only in the kerygma as a word of forgiveness of sins. It is important that forgiveness is here conceived of as an act, and that the onesided Barthian view of the Word as transmitting knowledge is eliminated.

At another point in the New Testament anthropology, parallel to the doctrine of sin, Bultmann does not maintain a comparable thesis, viz., the New Testament teaching about death. For such teaching we find no support in the philosophy of existentialism. We must again make a leap into the kerygma. According to the New Testament death does not belong to man's nature; it is, as Bultmann himself points out, something which comes from sin, from that universally enslaving power which man by himself cannot perceive (Rom. 5:12). Neither can man recognize death as a foreign tyrant; it appears as "nature." He would be able to recognize death as a tyrant only from a point outside of the ego, from a point where deliverance has occurred and death is vanquished. This point —and here we arrive at our principal objection to Bultmann—

is given in and with the New Testament kerygma. From the philosophical point of view there is nothing more offensive in the doctrine of death than in the doctrine of sin. If we have made a leap into the kerygma at one point, we have to make it also at the other point. Forgiveness of sin as an act of God is just as unacceptable as resurrection viewed as an act of God. Both of these points belong to the kerygma which is the proclamation of the death of Jesus on Golgotha, and his resurrection on the third day, and which as such is the gospel of the forgiveness of sin. We cannot prove the truth of either one. To bring in a proof would deprive the kerygma of its character as proclamation. In both cases the New Testament word produces, or rather implies, a judgment on self, a judgment of the ego in its totality as enslaved and surrounded by two enemies, sin and death. It can attain its freedom only by two divine acts: forgiveness of sin and resurrection from the dead.

Although we have maintained against Bultmann that the doctrines of forgiveness of sin and the resurrection are from a philosophical point of view similar, we might modify this statement to the extent that they are similar when confronted with a philosophy which applies a strictly objective analysis. But when these two doctrines are confronted with the philosophy of Heidegger, the situation changes. Sin might then be regarded as an intensification of the lostness (*Verlorenheit*) of which also Heidegger speaks. If we limit the redemptive work of the gospel to the forgiveness of sin, we can identify the righteousness given in the gospel with that "authentic being," "the real existence," which such an existentialism can very well recognize. The only thing that breaks the philosophical framework is the fact that theology insists on a word of hearing, a proclaimed word, out of which I find myself. If we extend the redemptive work of the gospel to include death also, assuming an "act of God" which breaks the power of sin, the whole analysis of existence by Heidegger breaks down. Human existence, according to Heidegger, is "being for death" (*Sein zum Tode*). We shall return to this point, but here we may anticipate by stating: Bultmann's treatment of the resurrection is completely dependent on Heidegger's treatment of death. At this central point anthropology places hermeneutics in a vise.[14]

It is remarkable that without abandoning Heidegger's analysis of existence we can think of man's existence as open toward and culminating in death, and in this sense limited by death; and at the same time think of man's choice of "authentic being" as a passing from "death" to "resurrection," or, in terms of traditional theology, from "the old man" to "the new man." Existentialism seems to be an abbreviated Christian view, a dogmatics without God and without eternity. But even if it concentrates everything within the short span between a man's birth and his death, it nevertheless conceives of "being" and "existence" as if man were on the way to something else than death. Just this that in "the decision" man has his "authentic being" before him, just the peculiar part which the term "future" (*Zukunft*) plays, makes it possible to take this philosophical vocabulary and insert into it an abbreviated and compressed content of the New Testament. The whole eschatology

[14] Since Bultmann does not recognize the resurrection from the dead as an independent, divine act after the act of forgiveness of sin, but conceives of the divine act as complete in forgiveness which belongs to the present not the future, we might describe the whole program of Bultmann's demythologizing by saying that the present absorbs the future. The whole program of demythologizing is already given in realized eschatology. This is especially clear in his interpretation of the Gospel of John; for instance, his opinion that John 5:28 and 6:54 have been added by a later redactor.

can be included in "the decision." The future is drawing near, in my "decision" I open myself to it, and the past (*die Vergangenheit*), "the old man" I throw away. We can accept this philosophical anthropology in the form developed already by Heidegger and find in it a death and a resurrection, a death and a resurrection entirely within human existence (*Dasein*); we can find an old and a new man. Afterwards we can go to the New Testament kerygma which has its center in a death and resurrection, in the death and resurrection of Christ, and interpret this kerygma existentially or anthropologically; i.e., as a death and resurrection of man. This, as we shall see later is actually done by Bultmann.[15] In this way Bultmann returns to the anthropology taken over from existentialism, but which now by way of the kerygma has become New Testament anthropology.

The content of this anthropology, the understanding of existence, is not specifically derived from the New Testament. Philosophy knows the same thing as the New Testament knows. But to know, to recognize, is not the same as to attain. One insight alone is new, the insight into man's bondage and sin. Here the New Testament brings something new into anthropology. Over against bondage on the anthropological side stands the act of God on God's side. But if this act is to meet man in the present, it must itself be in the present, independent of the past. The act of God must be totally in the present. It does have this character. God's act is comprised in the word proclaimed to me now. "Jesus Christ meets us in the word of preaching and nowhere else." [16] When the word is heard, I cannot go back in time and find out if the word rests on fact—that would be to flee from "the decision." Nor

[15] *Ibid.*, pp. 38-43.
[16] *Ibid.*, p. 41.

can I go forward into the future to a coming, eternal kingdom which would replace the uncertainty of the present—that would be to flee from "the decision." I stand in the present, and alongside of this present there is no other way except the way to unauthentic being and false security. Nor is there any need for another way.

Preaching is in the present, and this is the only form in which Christ comes, the only form in which the eschatological future is present. The word which I now hear *is* "the deed of God," the power which produces my authentic being. It speaks of "death" and "resurrection," but not of a distant death and resurrection, but of a death and resurrection which occurs now—my own death and resurrection accomplished by the word in which Christ dwells. This characteristic of the kerygma as being present is an important factor that permits the kerygma to be interpreted existentially. The attempt to go back to the occurrence of the event, to a past history, abrogates the kerygma, because the kerygma is a call. The attempt to go back and ask for facts also abrogates the decision of the hearer. He is then placed in the role of a spectator, and thereby the decision becomes impossible. Rather, the decision has then already been made. He has chosen unauthentic life. The whole content of the New Testament is present only as the preaching is heard now, demanding a decision. The Word is not found anywhere outside of preaching.

It is often said, somewhat by way of caricature, that the Roman church has usurped the place of Christ. It is not necessary to go back to the New Testament because the church teaches the truth in the present through its hierarchy. It is further said, also somewhat by way of caricature, that the Roman church anticipates eternity: in it the consummation already has been realized. The church is present, and the power of Christ and the glory of heaven are present in it. Now, if we substitute "preaching" for the word "church," we have Bultmann's conception; and then it is no longer a caricature but an exact description. According to him both what has happened in the past and what is expected in the future can be eliminated as essential factors. Both are poured into and comprehended in the kerygma. Here in the present lies their significance. Everything exists for the human being (*Dasein*), for the man who hears the proclaimed word; and being (*Dasein*) exists only in the present, in the moment of decision.[17]

Parenthetically we may point out that on the basis of this fundamental conception an entirely special way of reading the Bible emerges. Scripture is read as a precipitate of the sermon, as a proclaimed word, an address. It it not a question about a certain type of religious statements, as in Nygren's work. Nor do the scriptures furnish an answer to the question of knowledge, as with Barth. The active character of the scriptural word is very strongly emphasized.

When we, as we have done so far, focus attention on Bultmann's anthropology, the influence of Heidegger takes on special significance. Heidegger already played an important part at an early point in Bultmann's writings, and it is to Heidegger's *Sein und Zeit* of 1927[18] that we are constantly referred. We may discover this influence even in passages

---

[17] R. Bultmann, *Glauben und Verstehen* I, 146 ff. "The genuine form of the realization of the historical event of Jesus is therefore not the historical remembrance and reconstruction, but the proclamation. In it there is a twofold presence: Jesus returns and he continually returns. 'I will pray the Father and he will give you another Counselor' (John 14:16). The Counselor who continues the revelation of Jesus in the world is the Word proclaimed in the congregation. His teaching succeeds that of Jesus." It should be noted that the Gospel of John is the chief source of Bultmann's theology.

[18] M. Heidegger, *Sein und Zeit (Jahrbuch für Philosophie und phänomenologische*, Forschung 8) (1927), Vol. I.

where Heidegger's name is not mentioned. Barth's initial criticism dealt with Bultmann's dependence on the anthropology given in a particular philosophy. Most of those who have questioned Bultmann's conception on this point have expressed the same opinion. According to Bultmann's interpretation the proclaimed word has no other content than my own "authentic being" in the sense in which Heidegger uses that concept. There is only one item in Bultmann's presentation which is new in reference to the philosophy of existentialism, and that is the hearing, the listening to a kerygma, a call. But the originality is greatly reduced by the fact that Heidegger also describes man as "listening" in the moment of decision. Being (*Dasein*) hears itself call. This does not, of course, imply an audible, external preaching. But the way in which the sermon conveys the real existence to man becomes analogous to the manner in which in general "authentic being" reaches man.

This point in Heidegger's philosophy is connected with his view of how man loses himself. *Dasein*, i.e., man, can speak. Speech differentiates man from other beings. What is spoken and repeated and continually heard we repeat with our own mouth for no other reason than that it has been spoken. The universal speech which surrounds every growing child and which every one appropriates Heidegger calls "talk" (*das Gerede*). We never perceive facts which we might afterwards describe as reality in words. Rather, we first grow into this unfounded talk, after which we attain to truth on certain points in spite of it. To reach truth is to remove untruth, it is something privative, "*a-lētheia*." It is inevitable that man appropriates what "they" say, but this implies also that man loses himself in this universal "they." On this basis we can understand that the self, when it becomes authentic, appears as a "call." It is a call, a voice, because man understands him-

58

self in the midst of this "talk," in the midst of what "they" say; i.e., the "talk" is quieted down, man ceases to listen to his environment. What he then hears is "conscience." "In conscience, being calls to itself." "Das Dasein ruft im Gewissen sich selbst." [19]

The positive and valuable part of this reasoning could be that the accent falls on guilt. Man is conceived of as guilty and as recognizing his guilt. This insight is very important in our time when most theological mistakes occur because of the failure to recognize guilt. Theology is guided by a common view of the world which is characterized by moral relativism. The result is that the Bible is read as a book of norms rather than as a book of gospel. Moral relativism leads to biblical legalism. Bultmann is very free from such legalism because he sees guilt as something connected with human existence itself. Unfortunately he calls this which exposes the unbelieving man's precariousness (*Fragwürdigkeit*) "natural theology." "Even natural theology discloses how far unbelieving existence and understanding of self is governed and moved by its precariousness, which as such becomes revealed first in the Christian understanding of man. Conscience, for instance, is interpreted in this manner. This corresponds to the fact that the Christian kerygma addresses itself to the conscience (II Cor. 4:2). Just on this account the kerygma is a call to decision, and faith is decision." [20] No doubt systematic theology has something to learn from Bultmann here. However, Bultmann's own development of the idea of guilt only serves to emphasize that man's "authentic" existence, man's own life, remains central. Guilt is lack of self-realization, just as salvation is self-realization. Again, Heidegger's influence is obvious.

[19] *Ibid.*, p. 270 f.
[20] *Glauben und Verstehen, op. cit.*, I, 161.

Heidegger himself talks about guilt. "The human being" is characterized as "fallen" (*Verfallenheit*), but we must not confuse this fallen state with "a fall" from an original condition. The human being has not fallen from or out of something, nor in relation to anything else, but exclusively from itself. And when conscience restores the self (*Dasein*), man is not called back to any norm or to "a better self" conceived of as some substance in man; but he is called back to self, i.e., to a situation of free choice, to his "possibilities," to this "choice," without having anything over, under, or in himself. If we take this absence of norms seriously and conceive of man's nature as contained in the choice, we arrive at guilt as Heidegger interprets it. The choice does not make that which is chosen "right." To think of "rightness" in these terms would introduce an objective and concrete norm. Naturally the choice cannot make that which is not chosen "right." There was something which I rejected, and the "not-chosen" is simply gone without any key to determine whether that which was rejected was something which I ought to have chosen or not. Life goes on with choice after choice, continually precarious, continually guilty. We can say of Bultmann's and Heidegger's "decision" what we said of Nygren's "validity" and "personal decision"; the choice is necessary because the question is inescapable, that is all.

In general the comparison between Bultmann and Nygren is interesting. The latter maintains that philosophy has a purely formal task to define the categorical and fundamental question. "The answers" to these questions are found in history. Among these answers we must make a personal choice. A descriptive science can describe the answers, but it cannot decide to select one of them. Choices are made in the realm of the moral life, which science does not regulate. Bultmann can, just as Nygren, use the word "formal" to designate the philosophical analysis of existence. Philosophy cannot provide "a concrete ideal of existence" and say: you should exist *thus*. Philosophy can only investigate what it means to exist; the existence itself takes place in existential acts, which can become objects of philosophical reflection, but which are not in themselves of a philosophical nature. When Bultmann has so often been accused of taking "understanding of self" from Heidegger's philosophy, he answers that his critics have confused the formal analysis (which is philosophical and which he calls existential understanding) with the concrete choices (the several decisions, which take place in the individual's life, and which are called existentialist). This distinction in German between *existential* and *existentiell* is from one point of view similar to Nygren's distinction between "theoretical" and "religious," or between "theoretical" and "ethical." In this respect Nygren and Bultmann resemble each other: both want to base theological work on a philosophical foundation in order to secure a scientific character for theology. Barth has no such interest.

Bultmann's defense against the accusation that his philosophical anthropology enslaves the New Testament exegesis is not adequate. It is true that existential decisions are left free, but only within a given framework. This framework is defined by the philosophical analysis. Heidegger's *Sein und Zeit* is used to furnish a universal and scientific knowledge about man's being, as Jaspers says, who asserts that Bultmann becomes blind toward philosophy because of his preoccupation with the book of a single philosopher. "His confining himself to a book by Heidegger and, as I suspect, his misunderstanding of this book because of his emphasis on its scientific, objectifying, and instructional character, means really that Bultmann separates himself from all philosophy." [21] However, for our purpose this is irrelevant. What interests us is another "block," another "blind-spot." Has Bultmann by his attachment to Heidegger arbitrarily circumscribed the exegesis of the New Testament? We must answer this question affirmatively. In relation to this question Bultmann's conception of death and resurrection becomes the decisive point.

At this point it is necessary to go beyond the subject of this chapter and to consider Bultmann's conception of scripture. In the New Testament there is a clear order of events: the death of Christ, the resurrection, and preaching (world mission). We must not reverse this order. It is clear that the resurrection cannot precede death. Neither can the preaching by the apostles occur immediately after death and before the resurrection; nor, of course, before the death on Golgotha. The proclamation to the world comes by inner necessity after the death and the resurrection of Christ, because then Christ sits on the right hand of God and sends the Spirit through whom the great commission becomes operative. When Bultmann considers these successive events, which the New Testament relates, he carries on a significant discussion about "concrete events" (*Weltfaktum*). "A concrete event" is one that is perceptible to everyone and can be understood under the category of cause and effect. Now the content of the kerygma is the death and resurrection of Jesus. The first is "a concrete event" perceptible to all men, the crucifixion of Jesus. The second corresponds to another "concrete event," the preaching of the apostles.[22] This means that the series of three events is

[21] Karl Jaspers, "Wahrheit und Unheil der Bultmannschen Entmythologisierung," in *Schweizerische theologische Umshau* (1953), p. 79.

[22] "The cross and the resurrection are different insofar as the cross is an ambiguous phenomenon. It is an historical event which can be understood as such, i.e., in the category of cause and effect, and as human

reduced to two: the death of Christ and the preaching of the apostles. The resurrection lies hidden in preaching. Preaching is the only form in which the resurrection of Christ is present and reaches the hearer. The resurrection is the cross of Christ proclaimed, a word addressed to me. "The faith of Easter is just this—faith in the word of preaching." [23] If we remove preaching, the death of Jesus would simply be the tragic end of a noble life.

Many noble men have died in the course of time. But after they were dead no preaching has taken place in their name. But after the death of Christ there was preaching of and about him. If we now try to find something unique in this Jesus which would justify this preaching, we would presumably search for and retain a mythological element. In case we cannot discover such an element, it becomes impossible to say why we should preach about him! We might just as well preach about someone else who is dead. It just so happens that we preach about Christ. The significance of preaching is to be understood existentially or anthropologically: the hearers themselves are to die and rise again; I am to die and rise again, forsake my old life, open myself for the future, for my real self. Only by understanding it this way can we eliminate the mythological element.

When we look at this argument as a whole, it seems inevitably to mean that the proper name Jesus, or Christ, or Jesus Christ is and remains an uninterpreted remnant of mythology

accomplishment or suffering. . . . Unbelief encounters only the assumption (*Behauptung*) that Jesus is risen. Just as in the divine judgment of the cross so also the divine act of salvation in the resurrection has its correspondence in an historical event (*Weltfaktum*) which is also ambiguous, i.e., the Christian kerygma." *Glauben und Verstehen, op cit.,* I, 208.

[23] *Kerygma and Myth, op. cit.,* p. 41.

(in Bultmann's sense).[24] This proper name never finds a place in the existential interpretation. The personal name marks the constant point of origin of the kerygma. That we continually return to the death of a definite person, the death of the One, and proclaim him as dying for the others, is a constant in the kerygma which, on the basis of the existential interpretation, is inexplicable. The kerygma might presumably sometimes change form, start with the death of someone else, or from the death which has taken place in all the hearers from generation to generation. But this is not done. The impulse proceeds from one single point: Jesus Christ. This kerygma itself is a mythological element (in Bultmann's sense), although the demythologizing scissor cuts in it but does not cut it out. Without giving any reasons Bultmann stops short of the kerygma, of one "mythological" element. And this he is not able to interpret existentially.

It is beyond doubt that according to the New Testament eternal life is bestowed through the gospel, which therefore is understood as regenerating and recreating. But this implies that some hope for the future appears in this present word (I Pet. 1:21-23; Col. 1:5, 23). Bultmann frequently speaks of the proclaimed word as pregnant with eternal life, but this means that life is here, everything is now realized. In this way the resurrection of Christ loses its independent significance and is absorbed into this factor of salvation history, the proclaimed Word. We may restate it as follows: The resurrection of Christ is not extraneous to preaching, but is contained in the word; the resurrection of the listener is not outside of the word addressed to him, but is contained in the word. If now this word, insofar as it is a word about Christ, the One, is a mythological element which cannot be totally interpreted existentially, and consequently "mythology" is inescapable, why should then the kerygma of Christ be accepted but his resurrection be eliminated (i.e., disappear in the kerygma)?

We have met this problem before. We have seen that Bultmann, in spite of his philosophers, maintains that sin is not a mythological conception, and that "an act of God" is therefore something which can be accorded a place in a demythologized theology. We have also seen that he refuses to apply this same reasoning in regard to death. If, as the New Testament teaches, death is a tyrant, the resurrection is nothing else than "an act of God" which restores man's "authentic being." The real authentic life is found only in the resurrection of the dead when death has been vanquished. To Bultmann this is a senseless statement. Whatever man's real existence is, it must be contained within the purely formal conception of existence developed in the analysis of the philosophy of existentialism. If the New Testament conflicts with this conception, the New Testament must retreat.

Here, as in the work of Nygren, it appears that the so-called formality is not formal at all but filled with content. It is in the realization of his own death that man attains to his authentic being. According to this philosophy a victory over death would be a fleeing from "existence." The kerygma may be tolerated, it can find room within the general framework: Being (*Dasein*) listens to his own call. But the resurrection destroys the very foundation of all existential interpretation. To make room for this part of the New Testament would invalidate this whole approach to the theological task.

CHAPTER FOUR

Review and Perspective

At this point in our presentation it is appropriate to review the anthropological presuppositions of our three theologians and to restate the results.

Anders Nygren thinks that the final result at which a critical philosophy arrives after it has analyzed religious and ethical experience in a strictly scientific manner is a formal, philosophical pattern without any kind of content. Positively stated, this means that as a result of the critical analysis the religious and ethical questions appear as independent and necessary questions. But the question itself is empty and without content. It demands an answer. The answers are found in history, where the actual religions and types of ethos contend with one another. A choice has to be made because the question to be answered is inescapable, but the choice has to be made without any assistance from science. Critical philosophy can only discover and define the empty question, the formal, categorical pattern. Scientific theology can only describe a given content, for instance, the Christian content, the Christian answer with its fundamental motif, Agape. The historical Christian affirmations, i.e., the statements in the New Testament, are regarded as "religious affirmation"; statements in which a religion or an ethical ideal express themselves.

In this connection "the law" presents a great difficulty. The New Testament message about God's love, God's grace, God's forgiveness, presupposes that the relationship between God and man on the basis of law and judgment has already been established and is valid when the word of the gospel appears. Agape left in a vacuum, without standing in tension with the law, is no longer Agape. These questions, especially the relationship between Agape and Nomos, love and law, will be considered in the chapter dealing with Nygren's motif research.

Karl Barth does not base his theological work on a special, philosophical method. He does not work with the concepts of "religion" or "ethical ideals," and he does not read the Bible or the New Testament as containing "religious or ethical affirmations." The Bible is a witness to God's revelation and contains God's word to man; a word that has become incarnate in Jesus Christ. Apart from Christ man has no knowledge of the God of revelation. This negative attitude to the natural knowledge of God is an important part in the Barthian anthropology. The word of the Bible imparts the knowledge of God which man himself lacks. This lack of knowledge plays a most important part in his description of man. The principal function of the word is the impartation of knowledge.

In this connection the law presents a great difficulty. If the law were already operating as soon as human life exists, and if the law were at the same time God's law, a part of the knowledge of God would actually be available before and independently of the word of Christ, the gospel. Since the specific function of the revealed word is to impart knowledge of God, which can be attained in no other way, the word would lose its unique position if such a law were really given. The word is one word, and in this one word the gospel is primary. The law is contained in the gospel. The order "gospel and law" becomes, therefore, imperative, and the traditional order, "law and gospel," must be rejected. We shall deal with the significance of this position of Barth in the chapter on "Barth's Conception of the Word."

Rudolf Bultmann agrees in a certain sense with Nygren against Barth; from another point of view he agrees with Barth against Nygren; and from a third point of view he departs from both Nygren and Barth. His position is, therefore, somewhat unique in modern theology. In the interest of clarity we will discuss these three points seriatim:

Bultmann and Nygren both accept a concrete philosophy and establish the scientific character of theology on a philosophical basis. The former works with modern, Continental existentialism; the latter with Kantian, critical philosophy. This involves dependence on a factor which might disturb the interpretation of scripture, unless this factor should prove to be completely formal. Both of them insist on the complete formality of the philosophical component in their own system. But in neither case does a critical analysis substantiate their claim. In reality the philosophy controls the interpretation. We may also say, of course, that Barth's negative conception of man determines his interpretation, but he is nevertheless not bound by a concrete philosophy.

Bultmann and Barth conceive of scripture as kerygma, an address. Neither one thinks of "Christianity" as one among many "religions." Nor do they hold that the theological task is a description of a given, historical "material." Both endeavor to give an interpretation of "the Word" in its significance for this age. The historization of theology, which has been the result of Nygren's influence on Swedish theology, is foreign to them.

From a third point of view Nygren and Barth stand united against Bultmann. The latter is the only one who regards man's relationship to the law as established independently of the kerygma, and assigns to this relationship a fundamental significance for his whole system of theology. Bultmann's vigorous emphasis on Christ's death and resurrection as the center of the kerygma, and his existential interpretation of this center as at the same time man's death and resurrection, cause him to accentuate the law. He does this in the order "law and gospel." Law, death, and the old man are synonymous. The gospel, life, and the new man also belong together. In a quite typically Lutheran fashion Bultmann develops his thesis of law and gospel (death and resurrection), and refers frequently to Luther's interpretation. The problems which Bultmann's program of demythologizing forces upon us are to some extent different from those presented to us by the theological work of Nygren and Barth. It is therefore convenient to ignore Bultmann's interpretation of the Bible for the present and to concentrate our attention on the other two theologians, Nygren and Barth.

It is, of course, true that all three of these theologians have difficulty with the concept of guilt, but this is especially true of Barth and Nygren. Bultmann's special problems are in a different area. The other two are especially vulnerable in their treatment of the law; a factor for which, because of the structure of their system, they have difficulty in finding a place. In fact, neither of them can find a place for it without a radical change in their whole method of approach.

If this problem were not so serious, our criticism of Nygren might be answered by arguing that our objections are purely theological, and that they concern his historical description of early Christianity but not his philosophy. If that were true, we should make a new and more correct historical analysis, incorporate Nomos into the system and give due recognition to the dialectic relationship between law and gospel. Even such an "answer" would then nevertheless be an answer to the fundamental question of religion. This line of reasoning might seem feasible, but it shows a lack of understanding of the real problem. In the first place, after the correction has been made, Agape does not become an answer to the fundamental, categorical question of religion, but rather to a question defined by law and guilt, a question which has a definite content. Agape is no longer then "a fundamental motif," for by definition a fundamental motif must answer a question posed and defined by philosophy. In the second place, if the law is described correctly according to content (i.e., theologically), it cannot be an answer derived from the historical material to the fundamental question of religion. This is, of course, how Nygren describes "the Old Testament Nomos motif" which appeared at one point in history and has ever since influenced subsequent developments.[1] But the law must be something under which man stands—as man—now and always. Any other description and any tendency to identify Nomos with ideas contained in a certain historical material are theologically incorrect. Just as we have maintained that Agape, when it is correctly described according to its content, cannot be a fundamental motif, so now we must affirm that the law, when described correctly according to its content, cannot be a fundamental motif. This combination of philosophical question and historical material which belongs by definition to a fundamental motif is not applicable in this connection.

In the case of Barth it is easier to see that the law does not receive its proper place within his system. With a loud fanfare Barth himself drives out the law from its rightful place, while Nygren just quietly defines "a fundamental motif" in such a way that the law no longer finds a place within the Christian

[1] *Agape and Eros, op. cit.,* p. 254 ff.

faith. Barth empties man of any knowledge of God in order to enhance the didactic function of the revealed word. This process of emptying is applied radically also to the law, so that the knowledge of the law is incorporated into the one revealed word, the gospel. The law must be derived from the word about Christ and is, therefore, secondary in reference to the gospel: *Evangelium und Gesetz*. In the next chapters we shall have opportunity to deal with Nygren's and Barth's conceptions of the law. For the present we are interested in defining the methodological problems which an analysis of the law presents. We limit ourselves, therefore, to this one aspect of anthropology, the doctrine of the law.

An ethic which is simply deduced from scripture must be rejected from the point of view of scripture itself. To derive rules of conduct from the biblical documents and assume that rules not found in them are therefore not good rules is to abuse these documents and use them for inappropriate purposes. It is indeed significant that such practices have obtained to only a slight degree during the course of church history. It is foreign to the exegesis of both the ancient church and to the Reformation. If we assume that the primary function of the gospel is to bestow righteousness and life on those who are subject to sin and death, it becomes rather misleading to insist that the law which compels men to do works must be derived from the word of scripture. It is misleading because it assumes that the gift of the gospel would be superfluous if man could do good works—as if righteousness before God consisted in good works. The tremendous energy with which Barth tries to eliminate the idea of natural law shows that he does not conceive of the gospel as bestowing righteousness but as furnishing *knowledge* of God and his will. This emphasis produces two results: the natural life must be drained of "law," i.e., of God's activity; and the revealed word must be filled with ethical content and thus lose its special character as an act of God, namely, the act of forgiveness. The world becomes profane, and the scriptures become legalistic.

Luther's doctrine of "the secular realm" is a part of his theology which helped him to assign a correct place to scripture. The part of his doctrine which appears most dubious to the Barthians—that the demands of the secular government are not derived from scripture—is one of the great advantages, and bears witness to Luther's unusual, intuitive insight into the nature of scripture. Luther starts with the Pauline summary of the law according to which love of neighbor is the substance and fulfilment of the law (Rom. 13:8-10; Gal. 5:14). He then finds the demands of love to neighbor expressed in the claims which life in a community with other people imposes upon us. In the sixteenth century these demands were formulated by "the rulers," "the princes." In this way the golden rule (Matt. 7:12) can become also the content of natural law. "So whatever you wish that men would do to you, do so to them; for this is the law and the prophets."

In the twentieth century these demands do not originate with "the princes"; but they are nevertheless present, because we, too, live in a community, and the same demands are placed upon us also in the modern community. These demands, inherent in community life, are for two reasons never in our time subjected to theological analysis. First, the theology which is now dominant has been influenced by Barth, and denies in principle the possibility of obtaining any knowledge of such demands. Second, the theology of the Lutheran tradition, which is to some extent free from Barthian influence, is tied down to an ancient conception of the community, the old division of estates or classes. The only solution is to detach

72

ourselves from the sixteenth century and undertake anew the great interpretation of scripture which Luther accomplished for his own generation. When we consider the Bible itself, we are dealing with the present; this present in which the neighbor and I live.

The Lundensian and the Barthian theology are alike in that they can easily accept statements that express such demands directed to us in our ordinary life, provided it is understood that they originate in and are derived from the Christian faith. Barth can speak in this way on the basis of the word of Christ which provides knowledge of God. The Lundensian theology finds it possible to use these statements because they are regarded as the expression of a religious and ethical point of view; i.e., the Christian.

There is an important difference between these two lines of thought; the one thinks of the word of the New Testament as an address, the other as historically given material. But on one decisive point they agree: the question of who speaks —the question of man—is in the center. In and by itself, it seems, there appears no bondage to law and commandment; no bondage of which we can speak in the same manner as this modern theology speaks of the New Testament word. Of this latter they speak without preliminary introduction. It is given (*vorhanden*). But man's subjection to law is not given or obvious. We must find a subject who "tells" us that man is under law.

But this separation between the law and the gospel is the work of a modern theologian. It is he who separates; "the Word" does not do so; the New Testament does not do so; the Reformation does not do so. And this separation, which originates in a modern world-view, changes the significance of the relationship between law and gospel. The assertions about bondage under the law become assertions on the basis of the gospel and of faith. By that method we can never produce a correct description of the relationship suggested in "the material," "in the Word." The question about knowledge assumes control. It is not possible to express clearly the living conception of the law as governing all men and actually in force even where no one says that it rules. Scripture presupposes that its word is addressed to a world which does not need the Christian point of view in order to understand law, guilt, and judgment. The world lives in this situation and knows that it is subject to these powers. The modern theologian wants to interpret the Bible on the basis of its own presuppositions, but at the same time he removes one half of these presuppositions.

We ought to realize that such a theology is new; it is really the product of the early twentieth century. It is contemporary with the relativistic conception of morality which characterizes modern philosophy. A student of the history of thought soon discovers how theology in the past has absorbed the contemporary world-view and incorporated it into the Christian faith which it intended to interpret. Theology of today is very likely no exception. Our present world-view enters by way of modern philosophy as a pregnant and disturbing factor into the analysis of the documents. In spite of its claim of being strictly scientific it is easy to discern the contents of its world-view. Formerly, up to the twentieth century, theology had at its side an idealistic philosophy. When it spoke about "the law," or "the good," it did not need to derive these concepts from scripture. It could point to something universally acknowledged apart from scripture. From the present point of view, when "the law" has become an exceedingly problematical concept, the old consensus in the sphere of moral philosophy might appear very favorable; and we might be tempted to regret its passing. But that is very likely a mistaken notion. From a theological point of view the former situation was just as misleading as the present.

Within the former situation "the law" was not overthrown. Within a system of natural law it is self-evident that the law is the fundamental framework. According to the New Testament "the gospel" must make the law antiquated, overthrow it, and vanquish it. It is easy to show that in an older theology, which still operated with a vigorous idea of law, the gospel was seldom allowed to overthrow the law. The event of Christ rather restored the reign of the law which had for the moment been upset by sin. Every age has its own difficulties in interpreting the Bible. A restoration of natural law might no doubt lead theology out of the ethical nihilism characterizing it at present. This nihilism makes the interpretation of the gospel difficult since the interest must be shifted from the question of guilt to the question of knowledge as long as this ethical vacuum remains. But a revival of the concept of natural law would very likely lead theology into other difficulties of interpretation. The idea of an immutable law which excludes an active God prevents us from conceiving of the demands of the law as acts of God issuing in works of man. In this connection it is instructive to consider Luther's doctrine of the law. The idea of an immutable and eternal law is foreign to him, but at the same time he is free from ethical nihilism. His conception of the law is an excellent expression of the biblical ideas of God and human fellowship.

Luther conceived of the law as active in the ordinary and actual duties of life. Man does not possess in principle a knowledge of the good from which he can eventually derive concrete statements that apply to a given situation. The God who acts and governs in the present creates these situations. And since the neighbor is present in these situations and in his needs calls on us, life becomes loaded with demands; the demands of the neighbor which are at the same time the demands of God. The idea of an immutable law, an order which has been established once and for all and functions by reason, nullifies, strangely enough, Luther's doctrine of "the secular realm." If there is such a law, there is no need for a God who creates in the present, only for a God who once set everything in motion. If God lives and continually creates anew, he cannot tolerate such a law or such an obstacle to his new acts. According to this interpretation of the Reformers the law becomes the sum of living moments, a continual pressure from God's left hand. The law does not bring the gospel or salvation, but it compels men to act and drives them into the state of guilt; i.e., it drives them over to God's right hand, which is filled with the gospel, and which performs another act—the act of forgiveness of sins and regeneration.

Quite a few theologians at present are of the opinion that Luther's conception of the law is correct and expresses faithfully the biblical doctrine of the law. If they think so, they ought at once to begin a study of modern, contemporary law and the modern community; or at least propose such a study as a theological task of highest importance. If they neglect to do so, they have thereby clearly affirmed that Luther's concept of the law is not feasible. The so-called Luther renaissance is, insofar as it becomes a substitute for the contemporary task, pure romanticism born of impotence. But to renew the Reformer's interpretation of the law cannot be done exclusively on the basis of a study of Luther, unless we assume that the Weimar Edition is God's word which we are now to proclaim.

If Luther's interpretation is correct, it implies that he correctly interprets the meaning of the *Bible*. A new interpretation for our time in our modern situation, disclosed as standing under the law of God in spite of all its worldliness, must come directly from the biblical documents. This "return" to the Bible has often been understood as an attempt to produce a biblicistic theology. But the most effective prevention of biblicism is no doubt the Bible itself. The law that these documents speak of is not a law that meets man exclusively in a revealed word. It is a law which governs everyone, even those who have not yet heard this word, and which reaches man in his intercourse with men wherever that takes place. God is a God who acts and who rules all activity in the whole world.

During the sixteenth century it was natural to find God's demands expressed in "the secular government." Literacy was low, and community life was primarily determined by the family pattern. In our day we ought to raise the question whether common ethical concepts might not also represent "the law." The close connection of the law with government officials might well be a feature characteristic of a certain period in the past.

When theology encounters a conception of natural or generally idealistic ethics, the problem is usually considered from two points of view. First, it is asked whether the conception is philosophically tenable, and whether there are scientifically valid reasons for accepting it. Generally it is assumed that no such reasons can be found. The conception is a matter of personal conviction. Second, we may ask whether this idealistic conviction agrees with the Christian ethos. An investigation discloses generally that the root of the conviction lies in Greek philosophy, and is, therefore, a type differing from the ethos of the New Testament. Usually no other points of view are suggested.

We must concede, however, that wherever this idealistic conception rules many selfish acts against the neighbor are prevented. In addition, many acts are encouraged which imply that the one who does them serves his neighbor. It is possible to consider this idealistic conception from a third point of view: not from a scientific and philosophical, nor from its congruity with the New Testament, but from the point of view of its social effect. We can think of this conception as a power, as a restraining pressure on the self, or as a compelling pressure in men's intercourse with one another. But in that case we consider this conception from the same point of view as Luther regarded the prince. A new interpretation of "the law" which would correspond to what "the secular government" was in the sixteenth century would not be confined simply to governmental factors.[2] In our cultural situation there are other factors which also function as "law."

It is a general weakness of recent Protestant theology that the question of the relationship between the Christian faith and culture is answered in only two ways: either a separation from and a "no" to the environment, or a surrender and a "yes" to it. A certain type of culturally interested Protestantism has given up the uniqueness of the gospel and lost itself in contemporary philosophies; another, a pietistic type, has erected a fence against culture and asked for nothing more

[2] Paul Ramsey, *Basic Christian Ethics* (New York, 1952). Ramsey draws an interesting parallel between social institutions and theories of social ethics. "The relation between Christian love and existing social institutions therefore may be summed up as the constant criticism and reshaping of the institutions of society in the course of using them. And the relationship between Christian love and *other theories of social ethics* may be summed up as the constant criticism and bending of these social policies in the course of using them." p. 349.

than to live unmolested within its confines. In spite of the fact that Nygren has devoted considerable attention to philosophy and Barth has shown a remarkable ability to connect his teaching with the contemporary situation, it must be stated that both of them by their interpretation of "Christianity" and "revelation" continue the pietistic tendency and reinforce its position. This situation is due to the obscure place given to the law in their systems. The meeting between Christianity and culture takes place in the law. We must interpret the significance of the law in order to describe this meeting correctly without either underestimating culture, as pietism does, or overestimating it, as some Protestants do. It seems apparent that in this area some great tasks confront evangelical theology; tasks which so far have hardly been noticed. In this book, which is primarily a critical analysis of three theologians, we cannot develop this problem further.

If we examine the different theological methods, it becomes apparent that the methods themselves are a part of a theologian's interpretation. When the methodology has been established, the real theological work should begin. The work has then been defined in the methodology as an interpretation of the biblical Word, or an exposition of what Christianity is. But in the establishment of the method, in determining how the work is to be done, the first confrontation of "Christianity" with "the contemporary scene" has already taken place. The interpretation begins when the cultural situation is defined and the problem is stated. It always involves an interpretation for someone and for something. The choice of problems which is made in the discussion of method involves a judgment, an interpretation of the contemporary, cultural situation in which and for which we intend to interpret "Christianity." The problem which is considered in the discussion of method is a necessary problem which must be worked over and over again, just as theology and philosophy must confront one another continually. But at the same time it is clear that the talk about *the* theological method obscures the situation.

There is no one theological method. Or rather, there is of course a theological method, but it serves only to exclude the really difficult and essential problems. When the theological procedure is conceived of correctly and realistically, it becomes entirely relative, adapted to a specific situation when certain problems are the object of discussion, and conforming to the procedure followed in other fields closely related to theology. To the extent that the procedure becomes absolute and claims to be *the* theological method for all time, the method becomes in reality a hindrance to a correct understanding of the theological task: viz., the interpretation of "Christianity" or "the scriptures" in a given cultural situation. The striving after one single method involves in reality a risk. In our present situation, when the methods are subservient to concrete, philosophical systems, and their proponents accuse one another of being unscientific, there is good reason for discussing the *problem* of method rather than the method itself.

These considerations are important for determining our attitude to the question before us—the problem of the law. We have found it necessary to maintain that man's bondage to the law and guilt is an anthropological presupposition which cannot be eliminated from the study of theology. If this presupposition is surrendered, the interpretation of scripture goes awry. A false anthropological presupposition results in a false hermeneutical presupposition. We have also found that older theology could make use of contemporary ideas of law without the necessity of deriving the law from the biblical documents. This was an advantage. But the disadvantage was that the law was not invalidated, and the uniqueness of the gospel was not clearly expressed. Finally, we have found that modern theology, under the influence of modern, moral philosophy, readily surrenders the anthropological presupposition that all men are subject to law before and independently of their hearing the gospel. When the discussion touches on law, judgment, and guilt, the modern theologian is apt to derive these out of the gospel or out of the Christian faith. This derivation makes the interpretation of the biblical word more difficult. It indicates a wrong method. This whole skein of difficulties prompted us to present the problem of the law as a fundamental problem of the theological *method*.

The only solution available is to start with the actual demands which community life imposes, not from any conception of moral philosophy. Such theories often have a great deal to tell us about the actual demands of community life, and we have, therefore, much to learn from them. That is, however, a special matter. We can learn from philosophy as from any other area of science—no more, no less.

Our special question here has reference to the presuppositions with which different theologians approach the traditional material of theological research; and, more accurately, whether in these presuppositions there is a content which makes our understanding of the material more difficult. It may be assumed that all presuppositions present difficulties. However we approach the subject, we bring along habits of thought which are foreign to the matter in hand, and which must be eliminated as the work progresses. If we start with the actual demands of community life, we must sift these demands in the light of the Word, just as had to be done with the many demands of "the secular government." The value of these actual demands is that the neighbor is always present in them.

The relationship to the neighbor is present from the beginning; it need not be deduced from faith or from the gospel.

In conclusion we remind ourselves of the anthropological starting point. The gospel answers the question of guilt and bondage. When a different conception of man's situation is adopted, and such an idea, for instance, as man's lack of knowledge of God becomes an essential characteristic, the understanding of scripture necessarily becomes imprisoned in a false, rationalistic frame of reference. This is the background of our argumentation about "the law." It ought to be emphasized that this is not merely a confessional Lutheran accentuation, as Barth maintains. We could just as well utilize other New Testament interpretations of the death and resurrection of Christ; as, for example, the rich cultic associations, the atonement, the High Priest, the Paschal Lamb, etc. Above all we could gather together the great number of narratives of sickness and healing which evidently have a deep meaning. Along all of these lines we could arrive at the specific character of the kerygma as a divine *act* which breaks down human bondage in various forms. All the various biblical figures express the conviction that God has created the world and man, that he continually creates anew, and that he governs the course of events in accordance with his will in opposition to that hostile resistance in whose destructive work man has become involved because of his sin. The sovereignty of the law is a direct result of the corruption of life.

As has already been indicated, we will confine ourselves to the question of the place of the law in our consideration of the biblical interpretation by Nygren and Barth. Even in our study of Bultmann this problem of the law will have to be dealt with, but then from a slightly different point of view.

PART TWO

HERMENEUTICAL PRESUPPOSITIONS

CHAPTER FIVE

Nygren's Motif Research

In the section dealing with Nygren's critical philosophy of religion we found that his critical philosophy and his motif research are inseparably connected. A fundamental motif is an answer in history to a fundamental question of categorical nature proposed by philosophy. The formal nature of this question implies that from the question itself we cannot derive any pregnant propositions of religious or ethical nature. The pregnant answers are found in historically given, organic convictions which are localized in time and place, available in written sources and available for examination by ordinary historical methods. But when the systematic investigator reads these sources, he seeks first and foremost answers to those fundamental questions which critical philosophy has defined as categorical questions: the ethical (the question about fellowship) and the religious (the question about eternity). The fundamental motif gives an answer to these questions.

When Nygren writes the introduction to Part I of *Agape and Eros* (1930), he steps over the threshold from philosophy to motif research. His first concern is then to insist that these two are rooms in the same house and that there is a connection between them: "a fundamental motif is that which forms the answer given by some particular outlook to a question of such fundamental nature that it can be described in a categorical sense as a fundamental question." [1] The Agape motif has

[1] *Agape and Eros, op. cit.*, p. 42. Nygren continues: "Quite early in

the peculiar characteristic that it answers both the religious and the ethical question. God is the love which descends into the world of sinful men and bestows on them eternal life. And human fellowship should be filled with that love which does not desire to keep everything for self, but to give freely and spontaneously.[2]

It is characteristic that Nygren in this presentation of 1930 maintains that Christianity changes the question itself. "Ancient ethics was dominated by the question of *eudaemonia*, happiness. . . . Now it is just in respect of this question that Christianity makes a revolutionary change; for Christianity consistently makes fellowship the starting-point for ethical discussion." [3] Since the category of fellowship is, according to Nygren, the formal ethical category, it implies that the ancient ethical thinkers had not been able to maintain the formality of the question, and that this ethic, based on the ancient Greek philosophy was philosophically untenable (and consequently not only "different" from the Christian). In a similar way the religious question is changed through the appearance of Christianity.[4] In both cases the question has been filled with a certain content because it has been contaminated by a philosophy dominated by a particular view of life. It is a dominant feature of Nygren's work that ancient philosophy in this way

the history of thought we find the great fundamental questions concerning the True, the Beautiful, the Good, and—to crown them all—the Eternal. For our Western civilization the formal statement of these questions was the work of Plato, though the materials for it were in existence long before his time. And great as the changes may be which these questions have since undergone, we can nonetheless say that we are still occupied ultimately with these same great questions today when we speak of the problems of Knowledge, of Aesthetics, of Ethics, and of Religion."

[2] *Ibid.*, p. 47.
[3] *Ibid.*, p. 45.
[4] *Ibid.*, p. 46.

becomes the object of criticism. He had expressed this already in *Religious A Priori*, in *Philosophical and Christian Ethics*, and in *Fundamental Ethical Questions*. In principle there is nothing new in his reasoning in the introduction to *Agape and Eros*. His thinking moves in the usual and familiar patterns.

In accordance with this program, as we come to the real theological work, we have to penetrate the historical material and describe it. Concrete types of religion and ethos appear as "answers" to the categorical, fundamental questions. None of these answers is scientifically accurate, but each of them can be described and each can be rendered in scientific language. We must note that these concrete types clash with and struggle against one another in the course of history. A right description of them must focus on the dominant factors in each type; those factors which explain the clashes and the mutual antagonisms. To find these is to find the fundamental motif in each type. There are several fundamental motifs. They are also incompatible. Nygren describes those three which have had the greatest influence within European history: Eros, Nomos, and Agape.[5] In this critical survey our interest centers around Nygren's description of the fundamental motif in primitive Christianity, the Agape motif.

The material in the New Testament contains pronouncements which bear witness to a theocentric religion. The description of Christianity as a theocentric religion is very clearly expressed by Nygren. At the same time he preserves the point of view which was established by means of his critical philosophy of religion. Theology, by virtue of its being concerned with a concrete historical answer, is an historical discipline. It is, of course, not prevented from expressing itself about the present, any more than any other historical study.

[5] *Ibid.*, p. 247 ff.

Insofar as the historical event which is being described extends into the present, the description will have to deal also with the present. Christianity which exists today can be described and examined in regard to its fundamental motif. But the most important point is that the relationship between the religious and the theoretical remains unchanged and unbroken.

The theological propositions are propositions about religion, about faith; they are theoretical propositions about religious propositions. Furthermore, the whole sequence of Christian proposition lies within a definitely religious context. The propositions found in the New Testament in the Middle Ages, in the Reformation, and in the present are analyzed in the same manner, but with different results. To take a New Testament pronouncement and ask what this means now, what significance it has as now interpreted for men, is a question which is foreign to Nygren's system. Consequently this question is not even asked as a question that has any significance for theology. But in the life of the church this question is constantly asked, and it produces contemporary religious propositions which theology may examine in regard to their fundamental motif. The specific association of scripture with all subsequent time, which rests on the fact that all subsequent pronouncements are interpretations of scripture, has no significance for theology within Nygren's system. A statement of scripture is "a religious statement" of the same kind as later religious statements.[6]

[6] This historical conception of the words of scripture and their incorporation into a pattern of history of ideas appear most clearly in Nygren's works at the point where he attempts to break with the purely historical point of view. Cf. his article on "The Old Testament in the New Covenant" in *En bok om Bibeln* (Lund, 1947). Nygren seeks to make clear how a word of the Old Testament can acquire a new meaning when it is read in "the time of fulfilment," i.e., in the new covenant. In that connection it is interesting to see how often the combination "Paul and

It is not possible, therefore, to ask from the point of view of the Bible what significance this scripture has as now proclaimed. This whole question seems to be a mixture of a religious and a theoretical question. And from the point of view of the critical philosophy of religion it is clear that this question is really a mixture of two questions which must be kept separate. But now we are discussing the adequacy of Nygren's method and of his basic philosophical structure. Anyone who in undertaking such a study simply takes the starting point for granted and presupposes the distinction between the religious and the theoretical, merely proves that he is unable to see the problem. If Nygren's working program is such that certain aspects of the historically presented word of scripture cannot be developed, it is unreasonable to regard his theology as "scientifically" more accurate than another theology within which these aspects can be developed without friction and without any loss of objectivity. When a wrong

Luther" occurs. (*Ibid.*, p. 98). Nygren simply describes a view of scripture which is found in Paul and Luther, and which can be historically supported in the case of both men as they stand on the same level in the history of ideas. That Paul is within the *corpus* being interpreted and Luther is without, is irrelevant. That the real theological problem concerns the interpretation of scripture now (when Luther's interpretation cannot be repeated) is not even hinted at.

Theological problems are solved by Nygren on the strict level of history of ideas, which he never forsakes in principle. This impression becomes even stronger when we follow the description of the Agape motif from author to author down to Luther in *Agape and Eros*. The Agape motif is really purer in Luther than in the New Testament. This is really nothing strange from the point of view of motif research. A motif which appears in a historical milieu which is dominated by totally different motifs may find it more difficult to preserve itself from foreign influences at the beginning than at a later time in the history of ideas. But the problem is that the writings of Luther claim to be purely interpretations of scripture. When the interpretation differs from the text, the critical problem must be concerned with the interpretation, not with the New Testament. If this is not done, it is strong proof that the dominant point of view is that of history of ideas.

presentation is regarded as "scientifically" more accurate than a correct presentation, the word "scientific" is used in a way that must be regarded as superstitious.

This form of superstition arises generally in theology when a certain philosophy defines without reference to the material how theology is to work in order to be scientific. Any departure from this philosophical starting point is then declared "unscientific," even if it can be shown that it results in a better and more correct description of the material, and that a correct description is impossible on the basis of the accepted, philosophical starting point. Jaspers maintains definitely that such a kind of superstition is to be found in Bultmann.[7] But a similarly wrong point of view is to be found within Lundensian theology. The fact that the "scientific" character is defined without reference to the material to be studied involves a distortion at the very start.[8] This distortion is inherent in the system and cannot be corrected within the system by a later incision. The only possibility of correction lies in a purposive demolition of the religious-philosophical foundation.

[7] *Schweizerische theologische Umschau, op. cit.,* p. 78 f.

[8] When Nygren speaks about science and scientific procedure in *Religious A Priori* and in *Philosophical and Christian Ethics,* he implies already his distinction between theoretic and non-theoretic experience. This is true everywhere. The whole pattern of categorically fundamental questions to which the historical material furnishes answers is given and ready when finally the material is brought in for examination. All criticism of the pattern becomes necessarily a debate about philosophical problems on the basis of the Bible, therefore a quasi-philosophy, or a religious argumentation in a theoretical problem. If we discover, however, that the religious-philosophical reasoning is in itself an empty reasoning, provided it is not regarded as eventuating in the program of motif research for theology, the situation is different. For in that case the only justification for philosophy of religion is the tenability of the program of motif research judged from the point of view of the material. Not all philosophy of religion must be judged in this manner, but Nygren's philosophy of religion must be so judged. Consequently it becomes vulnerable to attack in regard to historical and exegetical material.

The uninitiated might imagine that the whole problem is a question of the degree of exactness we try to attain. Motif research is supposed to be an exact form of research, while the procedure which draws a direct line from the word of scripture to the situation in which the interpretation takes place is rather inexact. In reality a rather high degree of inexactness is found in both of these procedures. We must remember that in both cases we judge a later situation, separated by centuries from the New Testament, on the basis of documents which belong in an entirely different historical milieu, i.e., the documents of the primitive church. This is the intention of motif research in principle. The tendency to select Luther as the point of orientation rather than the New Testament must be regarded as a departure from the program of motif research, a departure caused by the difficulty of maintaining exactness in following the program.[9]

It is obvious that such a discipline as church history works with a greater degree of exactness than systematic theology in all its forms can attain. As soon as the problem concerns a comparative examination of widely separated groups of material and involves a total judgment concerning them, it is meaningless to expect an exactness which is possible when dealing with genetic details. We have to ask rather whether there are real problems which the systematic theologian can solve with the degree of accuracy possible in his case, and whether these real problems must be left untouched because dealing with them appears from the point of view of another discipline problem-

---

[9] Connected with this change is also the acceptance of the results in regard to Luther which Nygren has obtained through his motif research. However, when this motif research is the subject of the discussion, we cannot deal with these results at any given point. Under all circumstances we are forced back to the source which Luther desires simply to interpret.

atical. When a geologist establishes a date, he does not do so with the exactness of the historian; and the measurements that an astronomer uses are much less precise than those used by an atomic physicist. Nevertheless geology and astronomy must continue working with their approximate measurements. There are problems with which they can deal and which must not be left untouched just because a high degree of accuracy cannot be attained. The total appraisal of various forms of Christianity is also a problem which it is unjustifiable to leave untouched. The Lundensian motif research is an example of how this total appraisal can be carried out. Its shortcomings appear when we examine critically its analysis of the material; that is, they appear on the historical level.

There are definite historical realities, definite elements in the structure of the biblical word, which become obscured when the biblical writings are assumed to contain "religious propositions" supported by a fundamental motif. But this way of reading the material is already required by the philosophical approach. From the historical point of view the most dubious element in Nygren's analysis appears in his treatment of *the law* in its relation to Agape.

In his presentation of Paul's Agape motif Nygren sets it over against Nomos and over against Eros.[10] But nowhere in his analysis of Paul does he intimate that the Jewish law must

[10] For the contrast with Nomos see *Agape and Eros, op. cit.*, p. 111 ff., and for the contrast with Eros, pp. 133-145. The conclusion is drawn on page 143: ". . . Paul has given the Christian idea of Agape its highest and, in a sense, final expression, and he has also clearly marked it off both from the legal piety of Judaism and from the Eros-piety of Hellenism. . . . in preaching Agape, Paul has to fight on two fronts. Of these the struggle against "the Law" takes up most space in his Epistles; but documentary evidence is not lacking, especially in the Corinthian Epistles, concerning the second front and the conflict with Hellenistic Eros-religion."

stand as a necessary background to Agape. This idea that Agape demands the law as a necessary background is of no particular significance in Part I of *Agape and Eros* in 1930. God's descending and freely bestowed Agape stands in contrast to the efforts of Nomos-piety and Eros-piety.

Later in Part II of *Agape and Eros* (1936), we read that the fundamental motifs, Agape, Nomos, and Eros, are all to be found within the ancient church. Only two men represent Agape: Marcion and Irenaeus.[11] In the case of Marcion, however, the idea of Agape appears with a certain "limitation." The good God who has revealed himself in Christ has, according to Marcion, not created the world and not given the law. The New Testament which conceives of man as God's creation in God's world and under God's law can emphasize much more strongly the paradoxical element in God's love which forgives the rebellious. "The whole point of the primitive Christian idea of Agape is that it is sinners God loves—that is, those who in disobedience and rebellion have turned away from him." [12] Within the system of Marcion no positive unworthiness is to be overcome and no opposition has to be broken. God is a stranger who descends into the world belonging to the demiurge and bestows his grace on the miserable. "For primitive Christianity it is his guilt that separates man from God, for Marcion it is primarily his misery." [13] Marcion knows as well as Paul that the way of salvation by law is a false way, and that the law in this sense has become obsolete, abolished through Christ. "But he then concludes

[11] *Ibid.*, p. 317 ff. and 393 ff.
[12] *Ibid.*, p. 326. Cf. p. 327. "Marcion's system is sure proof that if the ideas of Creation and Judgment are set aside, although at first sight this may seem the way to assert the idea of Agape in its purest form, actually the result is prejudicial to Agape."
[13] *Ibid.*, p. 326.

that there must be no further talk about law at all. In other words, he has attempted to transform Agape from a trans-valuation of existing values into a new and permanent system of values"—and this implies, according to Nygren in 1936, the destruction of Agape.[14]

The weight of this argument is emphasized through Nygren's analysis of Irenaeus. Irenaeus holds that the saving God and the creating God are identical. This according to Nygren, tends to put greater emphasis on Agape. "Only when this unity is maintained can we comprehend the majesty of God's love." [15] Love is then directed toward the rebellious and guilty man. Nygren shows further that Irenaeus' central thesis concerning the reality of the incarnation over against Docetism has the same significance. (Docetism was also characteristic of Marcion.) God does not shrink from suffering; he himself enters it and he himself suffers. Finally Nygren finds this feature of Irenaeus' theology a third time when he discusses his doctrine of the resurrection of the flesh,[16] for the gift is a real gift only on the condition that the recipient cannot achieve it by his own power. The resurrection contra immortality is an expression of the fundamental gift motif, Agape. In these three points Irenaeus stands clearly over against Marcion. The latter is shackled at all three points by his separation between creation and law, on the one hand, and salvation and the gospel, on the other; and as a result he deprives Agape of its essential characteristic. In this connection it is peculiar that Nygren maintains that Marcion represents the Agape

[14] *Ibid.*, p. 332.

[15] *Ibid.*, p. 399. Quoting Irenaeus: "He, the same against whom we had sinned in the beginning, grants forgiveness of sins in the end." But the condition for this is that before God appears in the gospel of forgiveness he has already appeared in the law.

[16] *Ibid.*, p. 407 f.

motif. He has this motif; but because he has it by itself, isolated and separated from the law, as it were, he really does not have it.

We have to ask whether this positive presentation by Nygren does not constitute a critique of his own starting point in 1930 and of his conception of "fundamental motif" in general. A fundamental motif is supposed to be the sustaining element in any system.[17] It is not possible to express this motif and at the same time weaken it because another factor, the law, has been removed. This other factor must then be an essential part of that which sustains the system. The characterization in Part I (1930) needs to be reformulated. There the law was not presented as a necessary background for Agape. But in Part II (1936), this is done; partly in the analysis of Marcion and Irenaeus, and partly in certain general formulations at the beginning of Part II. Thus in his discussion of the Old Testament and its abiding significance he says: "Secondly, to eliminate the Old Testament, even in the interest of the Agape motif, can easily mean weakening of the Christian idea of love. Agape must, it appears, be seen against its original background, the Old Testament Nomos motif, if it is to retain its seriousness and depth. It is essentially a transvaluation; it is the conquest of Nomos, and exists only in this tension. Agape is destroyed if, by the removal of the tension, it ceases to be an actual transvaluation and becomes a new, permanent scale of values." [18]

No objection can be made to these words. They represent an accurate, historical observation. But do they not invalidate

[17] *Ibid.*, p. 37. "A religion deprived of its fundamental motif would lose all coherence and meaning." The example of Marcion shows that when the law is removed the whole system loses its coherence and meaning.

[18] *Ibid.*, p. 256.

the very conception of fundamental motif. Agape is supposed to be "actual transvaluation," consequently a continuous event in which the law is overcome. Agape exists only in tension with Nomos, in the victory now being won. The law retains, therefore, a function in regard to man even after Agape has "overcome" it. This function is such that Agape must continually come and deprive the law of its power over man, because Agape is Agape only in the actual and continuous "conquest" of the law.

Every word here is a repetition of Luther's view of the law. The normal place of the law is in the secular government, where it continually rules over the external life, but not over conscience. No man stands outside the domain of the law; to do so would mean that he is not in this world. Even prior to and independently of the gospel the law compels men to perform their work. In this status man poses his questions; and into this situation the gospel, the kerygma, strikes and answers the questions about guilt.

This is the situation: the law continually leaves its proper place, the body, the earth, and moves into man's conscience, into his relationship with God, into heaven. The spiritual, vexatious "use" of the law usurps the place of the "civil" use. But the gospel forces the law out of the conscience in that it speaks the word of forgiveness. The gospel bestows a new righteousness which does not consist in works, but implies access to a kingdom other than the earthly kingdom of works. If Agape exists only in its conquest of Nomos, then it is an answer to the question of guilt. If the New Testament comes with this Agape, this gospel, to the man who listens, then the New Testament assumes that every man is ethically determined by and subservient to the law. The gospel is intertwined with the whole sequence of God's work to which creation and law also belong.[19] The New Testament cannot be excised from the Bible and placed over against Judaism and Platonism, for instance, as if all three of these religious, historical entities were characterized by their own peculiar, fundamental motif—Agape, Nomos, Eros—each answering the fundamental, categorical question of religion.

It may be said that Nygren's criticism of Marcion is a retroactive criticism against Nygren's own presentation of Agape in 1930. But that is not all. If, however, we do not look back six years to the older Part I, but move forward within Part II of 1936, where we also have a long chapter about Luther, we must ask the question how the exposition of Luther can be fitted into this new conception of Agape as existing only in the actual conquest of Nomos. On the whole, Nomos disappears from Nygren's work as soon as he has completed his analysis of the ancient church. After Augustine the three-cornered struggle has resolved itself into a duel; only Eros and Agape remain on the field of battle.[20] When Luther enters the arena, he breaks down Eros and restores Agape, but we find nothing here in Nygren's book about Nomos as a necessary background to Agape. We must also remember that, according to Nygren, Luther is the theologian who has expressed the idea of Agape more clearly than anyone in church history, and that in Luther's writings there is an abundance of examples of this combination between Nomos and Agape which Nygren declares is theologically correct; that is, contra Marcion. These ideas of Nomos as background

[19] *Ibid.*, p. 257. "Against such a removal of necessary tension the Old Testament stands on guard, as the controversy with Marcion made abundantly clear." Nygren observes these contexts quite clearly. Cf. A. Nygren, *Commentary on Romans*, tr. Carl C. Rasmussen (Philadelphia: Muhlenberg Press, 1949), pp. 140-143, and 427 ff.
[20] *Ibid.*, p. 681 ff.

occur incidentally in Nygren, but they cannot assume a leading position in the disposition, the outline, or the presentation. Strong elements at the heart of his system prevent this.

We have already pointed out that Nygren's ethics is a description of "the new man." His theological ethics has nothing to say about the man who has not heard the gospel, or who just now listens to it. This is due to the fact that the types of ethos, like the types of religion, are historically given. Theology describes either Christianity or else a different, given faith or ethos, found in other sources. In the former case, the gospel of God's Agape is the starting point. The Christian ethos flows out of the gospel, it is the ethos of "the new man." In the latter case, a different historical material constitutes the starting point. The formal question is open toward historical material of different types, but this very openness means that it is closed in other directions. It is impossible to produce a description of the ethical determinism of man in general as long as this specific combination of philosophy and motif research obtains. As long as this situation remains, certain definite questions are in principle excluded.

The formal character of Nygren's philosophy is in a deeper sense a lack of radical formality, i.e., the absence of postulation in the original question. The gospel of the New Testament, which assumes that every hearer stands in the situation of guilt and judgment as the gospel comes to him, is made to answer a question from which the idea of guilt has been removed. This is interfering with the material and changing it. But this is necessary, because the theological method here introduced demands this interference and this change. The combination of philosophy and motif research demands this violation of the material: "the question is philosophically posed, the answer must be derived from the given, historical reality." The categorical, fundamental question is posed philosophically but the question of guilt is not.

Let no one say: Of course the gospel is an answer to the question of guilt, but Agape—a word which we have chosen to characterize a historical phenomenon, Christianity—gives an answer to the philosophically posed, fundamental question of categorical nature. Nygren himself has effectively closed this way of escape in Part II of 1936. There it is stated unequivocally: Agape "is essentially a transvaluation; it is the conquest of Nomos, and exists only in this tension." The only possibility for Agape to exist is that Nomos exists, that men live in "the valuation" of the law, and that through Agape "an essential transvaluation" takes place without thereby establishing "a permanent scale of values." [21] Again it is stated: "Through the law comes the 'knowledge of sin' (Rom. 3:20), and only against the background of sin is the depth of divine love revealed as the paradox of real Agape. When this side of the matter is missed, then the idea of Agape is inevitably weakened; the gospel of the forgiveness of sins is lost, and there remains only 'the gospel of the poor soul,' *das Evangelium der armen Seele*." [22]

Agape, therefore, is really present in the gospel of the forgiveness of sins, and in that gospel the law is a necessary background. That which is forgiven is judged; therefore forgiving it has meaning. And forgiveness is really "an essential transvaluation" which does not establish "a new permanent scale of values." It remains that what is forgiven is evil, but it is a forgiven evil. Purity is not something which man possesses; it consists in the word of forgiveness addressed to man. If

[21] *Ibid.*, p. 257.
[22] *Ibid.*, p. 332.

99

the ideas about Agape which Nygren sporadically expresses in Part II (1936) are to be consistently maintained, the material in which Agape appears must be a kerygmatic material, an address, a proclamation to man as he stands under the law. But then the law must not be understood in the sense of a limited, historical material, i.e., Jewish; the law must be something under which every man stands as man, with actual demands placed upon him, which are not derived from the gospel, but given simply because he is a man existing on earth. If this were not true, then Nygren's thesis would imply that a man would have to become a Jew in order to become a Christian; an idea which on good grounds he has rejected in various contexts.

The anthropological and hermeneutical presuppositions implicit in Nygren's method lead naturally to the thesis that Marcion represents the Agape motif. This is clearly Nygren's opinion. But if there is anything which differentiates Nygren from Barth and Bultmann, it is his more accurate historical observation and his reluctance to use extravagant, historical reconstructions. His thesis that Marcion is unable to express the content of Agape and his contention that Agape exists only in the continual tension with Nomos rest on purely historical observation. This is simply a description of the gospel in its kerygmatic character, and implies a disintegration and a breaking up of the old anthropological and hermeneutical presuppositions in his method.

The new thoughts can therefore not gain ground. They appear momentarily in the analysis of Marcion, but they have no part in the presentation of Luther a few hundred pages later in the same book.[23] They invalidate the very conception

[23] In Nygren's writings during 1940-50 the doctrine of the two ages (aeons) plays a prominent part. This is a significant reorientation which

of a fundamental motif and finally abrogate his critical philosophy of religion. If Nygren's analysis of Marcion is correct—and it is—we must give up and reject the combination of a philosophical question and an historical material, which is the very center of his system. If Agape exists only in the tension with Nomos, as Nygren indicates in his analysis of Marcion, then neither Nomos nor Agape are fundamental motifs in the sense in which he defines it in his discussion of method.[24]

In the previous chapter, "Review and Perspective," where we summarized the discussion of the anthropological presuppositions, we found that the law is an ambiguous entity in much modern theology. It is necessary to *start* with man's subservience under the law in one way or another, to make this the point of departure, and approach the biblical material from this point of view. Nygren's discussion of Agape as existing only in the actual conquest of Nomos seems to corroborate this idea. The gospel is a word which is proclaimed in a world where the law rules. In the centuries between the time of the apostles and our time it would be difficult to find a better interpretation of this biblical perspective than

makes a more positive treatment of the law possible. The separation between law and gospel is here moved over to some extent to the tension between "the old age" and "the new age." But the former negative attitude to the law and his tendency to over-emphasize the ethos of the "new" man remains here also, and expresses itself in the very strong accent on the obsolescence of the old age: the new has come. See *Commentary on Romans, op. cit.,* pp. 206-224. This feature of Nygren's theology is closely connected with the elements we have noticed here.

[24] When Bring seems to assume that a closer analysis of the relationship between Nomos and Agape could be undertaken as an extension of Nygren's program, he fails to consider how serious Nygren's conception of Agape as "essential transvaluation" really is. This demands a different method than that proposed by Nygren. Within that method his talk about "essential transvaluation" is a sporadically appearing element which contends with the total presentation. Cf. R. Bring, "Anders Nygrens theologiska gärning," *Sv. Teol. kvartalskr.* (1940), s. 320.

in the Lutheran doctrine of the two realms. Here the law in the form of the secular order embraces the whole of human existence, while the preaching or the spiritual order denotes the coming of another world, another kingdom, which, as long as this world of law exists, is only proclaimed in the Word, but which later, in the resurrection of the dead, supersedes and replaces the world of law.

This implies that the definite victory of the heavenly kingdom, of Agape, and the abrogation of Nomos, *Lex*, belong to eternity where we shall see God face to face and no longer meet him through the medium of the word, the sermon, or hearing. As long as that condition is not attained, man stands here on earth in his calling, subject to claims and demands, and occupied with his work. About heaven he hears only in the gospel, in a word that is proclaimed. In this situation Agape can be "essential transvaluation," and it is so continually until death, without therefore becoming "a new, permanent scale of values." When the new, permanent scale of values arrives, then the time of this world is at an end; and with that ends also the time of the gospel and of the *proclaimed* Agape. Only if we conceive of the word in which Agape appears as an address, a proclamation to men, is it possible to maintain and develop the points of view which Nygren himself has suggested. But along the line of motif research and under the constraint of a critical philosophy of religion it is not possible to proceed. In this sense the system is closed—and locked to wrong results which at essential points clash with the material.

There is no question but that Nygren is right when he says that the Old Testament is a protection and a help against Marcionism.[25] This is not because the law is incorporated in

[25] We must note that the result which immediately agrees with Nygren's starting point is that Marcion represents the Agape motif. His findings

the Old Testament, so that we have to go to the Bible and find the law. We do indeed meet the law in the Bible. The law is God's judging and compelling will in respect to sin and the destruction of life, and this will meets us wherever God acts. But the biblical books have not been written in order that we should learn to know the law. In that case the Bible would simply tell us something that we already knew before, independently of it. The intention of the Bible is that a very definite sequence of events is to be proclaimed to men who are not able by themselves to appropriate God's redemp- tive activity, prepared throughout the Old Testament and finally culminating in the kerygma of the death and resurrec- tion of Christ which marks the culmination of the biblical record. The Old Testament together with the New Testament enables us to see that the events related in the New Testament are events which are inseparably connected with that original event recorded in Gén. 1-3 which concerned humanity as a whole.

Since these New Testament events are so closely connected with humanity, they also belong to humanity. As soon as they have happened, they must be proclaimed to every human being—and the kerygma is simply the peregrination of these events to the ends of the earth. The culmination of the New Testament is the preaching, i.e., world mission. And Agape appears in this word, in the kerygma, not in any other word. The movements of this word are the movements of the gospel, which take place in a world ruled by law where men are compelled day by day to work and act. The kerygma contains that which will be "the consummation"; in it lies the realm of resurrection which now is offered as a gift to him who hears.

that Marcion does not represent it do not agree with his starting point. It constitutes a criticism of the starting point itself.

And consequently, when such a word is proclaimed in this world of law, it can be nothing else than "an essential transvaluation," never "a permanent scale of values."

It is important to reinterpret "the law" in such a way that it represents the actual restraints under which men live. Law is oppression, compulsion, coercion, guilt. Men have always lived under such constraints, and therefore they have always understood the gospel. If this were not so, it would be a psychological riddle how the gospel ever could have been understood. Today, too, men live under such constraints, and consequently they understand when the gospel is proclaimed.

Our problem is that theology obscures this situation. On the one hand, theology operates with a conception of law which is dominated by the epistemological question, and which makes it necessary to minimize the constraints and regard them as theologically irrelevant. On the other hand, theology may operate with a conception of law as restraint, a law conceived as active. This in itself is biblically correct, but the "constraint" is exercised by the prince, the king, the parents, etc. For the modern man these do not exist and cannot exercise the restraint. This is the romantic attitude, a repristination of the fifteenth century. In the meantime the law functions in actual constraints, but it is not described in the way in which it functions. A reinterpretation of the law in our time would correspond to "the secular government" in Luther's conception, but it would nevertheless have to be something entirely different. It would contain a variety of ethical viewpoints which in the present actually express the law. The chief concern is to find the ways in which the demands of the neighbor assert themselves in our human community and determine life. When these ways have been discovered, it is important to realize that it is impossible to limit theology to purely historical tasks. Nygren's idea of the gospel as "essential transvaluation" breaks down the historical character of theology.

It is evident that historical research remains as an essential part of the systematic work which aims to interpret the Christian message. Hardly any basic, theological view is so dependent on historical analysis and reflection as the view that is oriented toward the kerygma. Its center is a concrete message which can be defined on the basis of the biblical sources. This kerygma assumes that the hearers live under restraints which of necessity change from time to time, and thus alter the situation to which the kerygma addresses itself. The kerygma itself must therefore assume different forms, and change becomes the necessary mark of the correct interpretation of the biblical word.

Let us again select Luther as an example. Our point of view implies that his combination of the secular order (law) and spiritual order (the gospel) was a good and clear exposition of the primitive, Christian kerygma, and that his interpretation is a typical product of the sixteenth century, tied to the sixteenth-century situation, and inseparable from that situation. These two statements are not mechanically co-ordinated, nor are they mutually contradictory. We do not mean that Luther's interpretation was a good exposition of the original kerygma, *but* unfortunately also tied to the cultural situation of the sixteenth century. On the contrary, these two elements belong organically together. Just because his interpretation was good and faithful to the original, it bears for all time the mark of the sixteenth century, and cannot be repeated in another time without losing the original meaning.[26]

[26] A systematic theology which limits itself to historical problems and regards their solution as essentially systematic solutions is historically blind. A clear acceptance of the fact that all previous interpretation is

There is no view of the history of Christian ideas (the history of interpretation) which is so eminently historical as the one we have presented here. The Reformation doctrine of the two realms is inseparably connected with sixteenth-century society. This connection with contemporary society made a real and faithful interpretation of scripture possible. The proclamation became a preaching of the gospel in the world of actual constraints. The gospel met the law and was found in the tension of a law that exercised constraint—a law that was overcome through the preaching.

This extremely historical point of view, which is simply the result of seeing the unity of anthropology and hermeneutics, necessarily excludes the possibility of regarding the systematic task as finished through historical investigations. Any interpretation which does justice to the biblical message is bound to its contemporary situation. If it is not thus bound, it is—considered as interpretation and measured according to the demands of the original—unsatisfactory. This is the situation in which systematic theology finds itself. Whether it defines its task as saying "what Christianity is," or if it sets the goal as an exposition of "the revelation in the word," or selects some other formulation of its work, makes very little difference. What is to be interpreted must in any case be interpreted in relation to something else. We cannot take over an interpretation from the past. Nygren's method of motif research, which is easy and manageable to employ, obscures to some

determined by its contemporary situation opens the way for systematic theology to deal with the present and the need for a new interpretation besides its work of analyzing the interpretations of other periods. These two tasks, the historical and the systematic in the proper sense, cannot without harm be neglected. They cannot be mixed together; they are two tasks. Exegesis cannot solve these problems, although its work contributes to the solution.

106

extent the really difficult position of systematic theology. It is not unfair, but rather true to reality, to say that motif research as a theological method actually prevents systematic theology from stating its problem in its most radical form. This is the principal objection to Nygren's method.

CHAPTER SIX

Barth's Conception of "the Word"

"The Word of God" is Barth's most central conception. His most important dogmatic work begins with an exposition of "the Word," an exposition that occupies all of fifteen hundred pages and is definitive for everything that follows. Before we can speak about God at all, we must discuss the means through which the knowledge of God is obtained. "The Word of God" is the only means. As far as Barth is concerned "the Word of God" is the only possible introduction to dogmatics. Nygren's attempts to find a basis in philosophy of religion are unacceptable to Barth. Nor could he accept Bultmann's philosophical anthropology. It is enough to know that man cannot obtain revelation from himself, and that instead he receives it from the Word. Dogmatics begins with "the Doctrine of the Word of God," and then proceeds to "the Doctrine of God," "the Doctrine of Creation," etc.

But in this doctrine of "the Word of God" the unexpressed presupposition in regard to the question to which the Word furnishes an answer would seem to become exceedingly important. We can even say that this presupposition is in reality definitive for Barth's theology. We could express this in another way by saying that his anthropology determines his hermeneutics. Even if the question concerns such an elementary, anthropological thesis—that man lacks knowledge of God —which, as we have seen above, is Barth's fundamental, anthropological presupposition, such a simple proposition involves

108

nevertheless a programmatic point of view for his approach to and interpretation of scripture. We intend to show in this chapter that this program is not in harmony with the intentions of the Bible, and that, on the contrary, it disturbs the structure and perspective of the Bible. In working this out we deliberately follow only very central lines of thought.

By way of summarization we might describe the situation as follows. Barth has a tendency to shift the emphasis in the gospel of Christ from the death and resurrection to the incarnation, the birth, the miracle of Christmas. When the death and resurrection stand in the center—as they do in all the four gospels and in the rest of the New Testament—the gospel has the character of a struggle. There is a kingdom of evil which must be destroyed, and Christ came in order to destroy it. (This destruction may be interpreted in various ways. That problem is not decisive in this connection. It is essential that one interpretation be excluded: the interpretation of evil as "Nothingness," *das Nichtige*.) Barth's propensity for concentrating attention on the miracle of Christmas depends on the central position given to the unqualified concept of "revelation." "God" reveals himself to "man," God appears in human form.

This shifting of the center in regard to the content of scripture corresponds to a similar shift in his anthropology. It is possible to retain the death and the resurrection at the center only if we think in terms of conflict and guilt, and therefore reckon with something actively evil in man; an evil that must die in order that a new man shall arise. In this view the death and the resurrection determine also the anthropology. Easter becomes the chief miracle, and the miracle of Christmas becomes a prerequisite for this supreme event, but not the chief event itself. But if we follow Barth in making man's lack of knowledge of God the essential, anthropological thesis, and also interpret evil as Nothingness, which only on the basis of an ontological misunderstanding can be thought of as existing, it is impossible to let death and resurrection determine anthropology. One result of this reasoning is that Barth pays scant attention to the contrast between the old and the new man. The old man dies and the new man rises again. This antithesis between the old and the new man stems from the fact that the death and resurrection of Christ stand at the center of the kerygma.

When the death and the resurrection of Christ have to yield their place in the center of the kerygma to the birth in Bethlehem, there occurs also a corresponding change in the anthropological conception. God's appearance in human form becomes the center of the gospel, and the primary function of faith is to apprehend this appearance of God in human form. Faith apprehends God and acquires knowledge of him—a knowledge which man did not previously possess. This dominant position of the problem of knowledge in Barth's theology appears in his emphasis on the incarnation as such over against the death and the resurrection. And the very same feature appears also in a totally different connection: the sequence, "gospel and law," replaces the order, "law and gospel." This latter sequence corresponds to the order in the events, "death and resurrection." The law kills, the gospel makes alive. This sequence becomes empty and meaningless when death and resurrection have lost their position in the center of the kerygma and have been replaced by one single event: revelation, birth, God's appearing. Then it becomes perfectly natural that the twofold "law and gospel" be replaced by "one single word," the gospel (which at the same time contains the law). These assertions, which have here been presented without any attempt at proof, we must now elucidate further in this present chapter.

The virgin birth plays a large part in Barth's doctrine of Christ. It is especially the element of human passivity in this event which is important to him. The birth in Bethlehem implies that God "makes room for himself among us," he enters in among us. The incarnation is the miracle. But this miracle has "a visible form." There is a sign (Zeichen) which points to the real miracle; and this sign is the nonparticipation of the man in the conception. "But we understand that it points to this gracious judgment (Gericht) of God when we realize that at this birth, without previous union of man and woman, man is indeed involved in the person of Mary, but just in her, in the Virgin. It implies that man is present here only as the nonwilling, nonworking, noncreating, nonsovereign man; only in the capacity of one who receives, who is willing and ready, and who can only permit something to happen." [1]

Barth, of course, does not mean that we could, on the basis of the message of the incarnation, postulate that this external sign, the miracle of the virgin birth, must be the visible form under which the incarnation appears. Such a demonstration would be contrary to the nature of a sign. A "sign," "a pointer," can be replaced by another sign, another pointer. But it is evident that he thinks of this sign as standing in an intimate relationship to the incarnation to which it points. And it is characteristic that the old enemy, "natural theology," appears here again as an entity that must be rejected. The absence of all human action in the conception, the pure passivity on man's part, the simple reception on the part of Mary,

[1] Die kirchliche Dogmatik, I:2, op. cit., p. 209.

designate evidently the same kind of emptiness and negation which is so significant for Barth's doctrine of the scriptural revelation over against the natural knowledge of God.

Barth's whole conception of revelation (*Offenbarung*) is clearly connected with his concentration on the birth in Bethlehem and on the purely receptive attitude of the human in the incarnation. The birth in Bethlehem attracts him like a magnet. Even in the New Testament there are examples where the incarnation stands as the central event in the drama of salvation. The prologue of the Gospel of John is the most obvious example, and Barth uses this frequently. But we ought to realize that the prologue is a prologue, not a complete gospel. In the Fourth Gospel, too, the essential content is the death and resurrection of Jesus. We know of no gospel, nor any other book in the New Testament, in which the birth occupies such a central place in the redemptive event as it does in Barth's theology. Even this matter of the proportions is significant. But the decisive element is, nevertheless, the overall perspective.

It is obvious that this concentration on the birth is closely related to the fact that in Barth's view there is no evil power, and that the two parties on the field of battle are just these two, God and man. In the birth of Jesus that which was not previously present appears. God enters the world of men. This fits into Barth's framework. God was unknown, but he becomes known through the incarnation. The death and the resurrection, on the contrary, are two entirely different events, following each other, and one is the opposite of the other. Death implies that the Revealer of God is crushed; the resurrection implies that he is exalted. This framework in which only two parties, God and man, have a place, but no active, evil power, breaks in pieces when we resolutely put the death and resurrection in the center and assign to the birth the position it has in the New Testament as the beginning of the work of salvation: (A beginning that quickly passes to the slaughter of the innocents, the flight into Egypt, etc., all of which speak of struggle and are precursors of the cross and of death). The enmity against Christ is a part of the total event. But this element Barth must minimize. The enemy does not exist.

It is, of course, true that Barth frequently speaks of the death and the resurrection of Jesus. But the frame of reference remains well defined, the incarnation is the chief event, and the general concept of "revelation" dominates the whole presentation. Nothing that Barth says in this connection invalidates his general principle that evil has no objective existence. This frame in which the enemy is missing surrounds everything in Barth's theology. It becomes necessary, therefore, to re-evaluate the events: the birth becomes the supreme event and stands in the center of the picture. The virgin birth as an illustration of man's passivity must appear as "the sign of the divine Agape." [2]

Barth operates in general with these contrasts: divine—human, absolute—relative, etc. We often find this dialectic in his interpretation of scripture. The word of the Bible is God's word, but it appears in the guise of humanity and relativity. "The human does not cease to be human, and as such it is certainly not divine. And just as surely God does not cease to be God." [3] But the human in the Bible can be "a sign," it can be "a witness." The sign and the witness are pointers directing attention to something else, something higher. The content of the divine Word is knowledge of God. If God nevertheless re-

[2] *Ibid.*, I:2, p. 210.
[3] *Ibid.*, p. 554.

mains hidden even in his word, the reason for this concealment is that he appears only "in the sign of the human word." The absolute reveals itself in the word, but when it reveals itself, there is still something human and relative in the form of its appearance, something which nevertheless hides the revealing God and justifies us in speaking about "distance" and "difference."

Since this idea of concealment governs Barth's theological system, and since he suggests no other theory or conception of this concealment, some very definite results follow. We might, of course, imagine that the content of the word is a gospel sent out to bestow righteousness on men, and that the concealment is a result of the fact that the word of the Bible at the same time demanded righteousness—a righteousness of works—and that the word would condemn man if he lacked this righteousness of works. In that case the concealment would imply that the gospel had its opposite—the law—by its side. It is not something relative that adheres to something absolute; it is something that kills which stands in tension with that which gives life, judgment in tension with grace. This conception of concealment Barth definitely rejects when he reverses the order of "law and gospel."

When the conception of scripture has the structure which Barth has given to it, our understanding of the function of the word as it reaches the hearer is very definitely affected. The conception of concealment which is connected with the tension between law and gospel, judgment and grace, implies that the function of the word is to kill and make alive. In that case we presuppose an active, evil power *in* the man who hears. Something has to be killed in order that a new man may arise. The law and the gospel are active powers, each one doing its own work in the hearer. Death and resurrection which the word

114

brings about are an outflow from the center of the kerygma, the death and resurrection of Christ.

When Barth rejects this type of concealment in the word, and rejects the sequence, "law and gospel," it indicates clearly that to him death and resurrection are not the central point in the gospel record. By systematic necessity he is drawn to the birth, the entrance of the divine into the sphere of the human. God "assumes" flesh, just as the divine Word clothes itself in human words; although the distance between the divine and the human is greater in the word of scripture than in the person of the incarnate Word. This conception of concealment according to which the relative adheres to the absolute, and Barth's typical predilection for the birth, the single miracle of the assumption of the flesh, both indicate that in the center of Barth's theology there is no enemy, no struggle, no death and resurrection. Rather, a God appears, reveals himself, makes himself known to beings to whom he was previously unknown. In order to do so, he must assume the appearance of those beings, take up a human form, assume flesh, and speak through external signs in the word of scripture. It appears clearly that there is an obvious shift even in the historical apprehension of what constitutes the center in the contents of scripture. But this interpretation rests on the anthropological presupposition. The decisive factor is that the man into whose world God enters through a birth and through the written word is a man without knowledge of God, a man without *contact* with God. It is not a man who is ruled and judged by God's law.

Man without means of contact with God is not the kind of man described in the biblical writings. This man without means of contact with God is the modern, atheistic man for whom the question of knowledge is the one essential question whenever the conception of God is discussed. In other connections this modern man can raise a number of questions of a different kind. Social life is filled with questions dealing with righteousness or justice. But in our day we do not combine the word of the Bible with this question of righteousness, or with the related question about guilt. Barth does not do so either. He is simply a modern man who takes over quite uncritically the general attitudes of contemporary culture.[4]

Whether this primary and fundamental "acceptance" of a question foreign to the biblical writings disturbs his work of interpreting these writings does not seem to worry him to any great extent. He accepts the modern conception of man as a being for whom God does not exist, and then he confronts this man who has no means of contact with God, who is ignorant of God and lacks all knowledge of God, with the content which he derives from the incarnation and the scriptures, *Offenbarung*. But in doing so he destroys the situation in which it would be meaningful to speak of gospel, forgiveness, and the bestowal of a new righteousness. In that situation the law must be the determinative factor.

In reality it might be possible to dig down to a point in the general, spiritual condition of contemporary life where this question of guilt and righteousness, which is the question presupposed in the biblical documents, is still a vital concern. It may appear in the guise of the twentieth century and therefore be difficult to recognize, but it is there. Without entering upon any analysis of the contemporary scene, however, it is sufficient for us as interpreters of these historical documents

[4] The sudden success of his *Commentary on Romans* was due to the fact that its fundamental conception of man was the conception of the post-war period. Nothing had to be corrected. It was possible to maintain the common understanding of life, but at the same time he was able to insert Christ and the New Testament into this framework in a new and novel manner.

to recognize clearly this one fact: We cannot understand or interpret these writings if we approach them exclusively with the question of knowledge. In the case of Barth this is exemplified by the fact that he is compelled to deny some elements in the Bible.

One of the most essential negations in Barth's theology is his denial of the objective existence of evil. This negative attitude appears in various forms. In this present connection it is most interesting to note his rejection of the two concepts—"the old and the new man." This dichotomy depends on the fact that the man who hears the word is conceived of as an actual sinner. Something old must die, something new must arise. It is also connected with the fact that death and resurrection constitute the center of the kerygma, rather than the incarnation by itself. And finally, this dichotomy is connected with the sequence "law and gospel." All these are elements which Barth in one way or another rejects. Consequently he does not like to talk about the old man in contrast to the new man. "Already the fact that they have to speak definitely about two separate, foreign and hostile beings indicates the confusion to which all these apostolic words have reference." [5] Barth is disturbed by this New Testament way of speaking, but he consoles himself with the thought that in his opinion the Bible "only seldom" speaks about this contrast between the old and the new man.[6]

According to Barth man as a creature cannot in principle

[5] *Die kirchliche Dogmatik*, III:2, *op. cit.*, p. 245.
[6] *Ibid.*, "We must note, however, that even the Bible speaks relatively seldom about this contrast." But in order to determine whether Barth's judgment about the frequency of this expression is correct or not, we must not confine ourselves to the passages where the words "new" and "old" actually occur. We must note the admonitions to struggle against hostile, evil powers, the words about the conflict between the flesh and the Spirit, and the possibility of falling away, etc.

stand in opposition to God's purpose and will as Creator. To be sure, God and man are separated and must not be confused. The One is in heaven, the other on earth. That is a situation which can be described in terms of superiority and inferiority. A struggle is something else, an active opposition, when the "creature" works against "the Creator" as an enemy. This cannot take place objectively.[7] An ontological mistake is, of course, possible. Man can act as if he had the power to campaign against God, and deny reality, even his own reality. This is "the insane possibility of sin."

As an illustration of this possibility Barth points to the passages in the New Testament dealing with "the old man and the new man" which we have discussed. In doing so his chief interest is in showing how confused this New Testament idea is from a logical point of view.[8] Thereafter he returns quickly to the main contention that in principle there can be no active opposition. It has to be possible to find in the human an analogy, a counterpoint, a likeness, which reminds us of and reflects man's divine destiny. After searching a while Barth finds such an analogy in the relationship between persons, expressed most clearly in the relationship between man and woman.[9] This specific anthropology replaces the New

[7] *Ibid.*, p. 244. "Man's divine destiny and his human nature as man are two different things as surely as Creator and creature, God and man, are of two different kinds. But they cannot contradict one another. They cannot separate one from the other, or stand in a neutral, exclusive or hostile relationship."

[8] *Ibid.*, p. 244. "And when we read in Col. 3:9 that we should 'put off' the old man and 'put on' the new, it is to be remembered that the one called 'the old' is in truth the one who appeared illegitimately instead of the reality, and insofar is the 'new' man whom we ought not to have 'put on'; and likewise, the 'new' man is in reality the authentic, the real, and insofar the 'old' man, the original man, whose 'putting off' we can only understand as the insolence of sin."

[9] *Ibid.*, pp. 264-391.

Testament antithesis between the old and the new man. There is no question here about a conflict between the good and the evil. The essential element is a chasm, an interval, a real distance between God and man; and, in addition, across the chasm a reflection, a reproduction of the higher in the dark surface of the lower. Everything that the Bible says is incorporated within this Platonic frame of reference which is never broken.

In this connection we must consider "the problem of address," i.e., to whom the word is addressed. Barth refuses to combine the doctrine of the word with the idea that the word is aimed at man, or is addressed to man, because in that case God's freedom would be lost. This is his argument in the first volume of *Die kirchliche Dogmatik* (1932), when he criticizes his own existential-philosophical approach used in *Die christliche Dogmatik* (1927).[10] This self-criticism is certainly correct. It is true that the word of scripture is addressed to men, but this is not a necessity based on the nature of the word, nor can it be deduced from the nature of the word itself. But what is debatable and interesting is just his fear and anxiety lest God's freedom and majesty should be curtailed.

This typically Barthian anxiety is caused by the fact that there are only two parties, God and man, and that "man" is conceived of as primarily lower than "God." If the higher being by his own nature is concerned with the lower, the order of rank is reversed. God's love could become a threat to his majesty and freedom. All these varied problems rest on the fact that in Barth's thinking there is no evil power holding man captive. As soon as we understand sin as a power, Barth's problem disappears. Then God's love for man implies a warfare, not weakness or slackness, or loss of freedom and

[10] *Die kirchliche Dogmatik*, I:1, p. 145.

majesty. And the enemy which is the object of the warfare is not outside of man, but within, in the form of the old man. If man is the one addressed by the word, this fact cannot give him a position of strength over against the one uttering the word, i.e., God, because the intention of sending the word is that the one addressed shall die—in order to rise again. Only when the empty question of knowledge becomes paramount can these specific problems which Barth deals with arise. The decisive point is that the law has been eliminated, and the question of guilt has disappeared.

A concrete example of Barth's concentration on the birth of Jesus is found in the part which Christmas plays in his theology. The miracle of Christmas (*Das Wunder der Weihnacht*) is an expression which he loves, and which occurs as a title in the important section which deals with "the mystery of the revelation." [11] In line with scholastic and orthodox tradition Barth makes the trinity, the incarnation, and the outpouring of the Spirit the essential elements in revelation. But here as everywhere else he lays special emphasis on the incarnation, *die Fleischwerdung des Wortes*. This is an element which appears in all his literary production. It is not accidental that one of his collection of essays bears the title "Christmas." But this exclusive emphasis on Christmas is theologically problematic. The birth of Jesus plays a relatively minor part in the New Testament kerygma. The cross and the resurrection dominate the four gospels, even quantitatively, while some of them do not even relate the story of his birth. Other passages which indicate something of the content of the kerygma confirm the central position which his death and resurrection had in Christian preaching from the very beginning. This has always been the central element.

[11] *Ibid.*, I:2, pp. 187-221.

One unique, historical factor, to which scant attention has been given, confirms the idea that his death and resurrection had the central place. In the first attempts to establish a Christian calendar, already in the first and second centuries, Easter is the first holiday mentioned, not Christmas. During the fourth century Christmas began to be observed; and its appearance is connected with the need of transforming a festival dedicated to the sun. Christmas is not a spontaneous creation by the early, missionary kerygma. Almost two centuries before Christmas was celebrated, the church began to observe the festivals of the martyrs, beginning already in the middle of the second century. These festivals were not primarily a remembrance of the martyrs as persons. They proclaim death as the form of existence of the Body of Christ, the way in which the congregation follows its Head through the cross to the resurrection. This is the testimony of the origin of the church year, and it bears ample testimony concerning the central element of the gospel. There is no indication that the birth and Christmas stood in the center.

We must note that all the factors which concern the structure of the church year are relatively late. It is, of course, significant that we hear about Easter already in the second century and Christmas only in the fourth century. But the real beginning is not so much related to the year as to a briefer period, the week. Sunday was a shock to the Jew. Sunday is the first day of labor in the Jewish week with the same connotations as our Monday. But it is at the same time the greatest day of joy in the early Christian congregations. Sunday is a continual proclamation of the message of Easter: Christ is risen. And Sunday is there from the beginning. It is mentioned already in the New Testament (Acts 20:7; I Cor. 16:2; Rev. 1:10).

But the Sunday commemoration of the resurrection does not stand alone. Suffering and death appear in the observance of "the stations." Wednesday and Friday were designated as early as the beginning of the second century as the two "stations" commemorating the betrayal and the crucifixion respectively. The whole week, therefore, is filled with the death and the resurrection of Christ. But there is no trace of Christmas. In this early period the chief content of the kerygma appears in the structure of the week, and later in the structure of the year, but the birth does not belong there. The birth is the beginning of the work of salvation. We must not minimize the message of Christmas. The frame within which Easter with its struggle and victory constitutes the center also has room for Christmas. What we must observe carefully is that the tendency to place Jesus' birth and Christmas in the foreground leads away from the New Testament.[12] When we conceive of the incarnation (*Fleischwerdung*) as the center of "revelation," it is quite certain that we understand "revelation" in a sense that is foreign to the New Testament.

The factors touched upon here also exercise a modifying influence on Barth's conception of the word as a call directed

[12] O. Cullmann, *Weihnachten in der alten Kirche* (1947) p. 27. "The question arises here as far as the Christian is concerned whether a special festival should be devoted to the birth of Christ, or if those ancients were right who rejected such a festival as un-Christian. This much is clear that the overemphasis on this festival in preference to Good Friday and Easter does not agree with ancient Christian practice, nor with the theological thinking of the early church. According to the New Testament the central event is the death and the resurrection of Christ. His birth must be viewed from that point, not vice versa." It is an important factor that in the church year suffering has received such a prominent place in the period of Lent, and that the Sundays after Easter deal with the resurrection. The church year has, therefore, about the same proportion of content as the gospels. But Christmas has naturally a larger place in the church year. There are many centuries that have left their mark on the church year, not only the first centuries.

to men, a kerygmatic word. In agreement with Bultmann and other continental theologians Barth understands the word as kerygma. This is much to be preferred to the Lundensian talk about "religious propositions." It may be that form criticism still exercises a good influence on continental, systematic theology. But the special feature of the call, that God is present and active in his word and deals with men through the word, is weakened in Barth's presentation. The dominant emphasis on knowledge results inevitably in an intellectualizing of the word. Added to this is the idea of a "sign." Everything external points away from itself. God is in heaven. He withdraws, as it were, from every outward form and disappears into inaccessibility. Nothing material is an organ, a tool, or a means which God holds in his hand and uses for his creative work in the present. As far as Barth is concerned this is true all along the line. The relation between man and wife, democracy, etc., remind us of the revelation in Christ, but there are no works of the active God in the present. Barth's indifference to history rests on this character of his system. But in this connection it is important to assert once again that this is also Barth's conception of the written word.

"God's acts occur with but never 'in and under,' always over and opposite to human action." ("Gottes Tun geschieht nie 'in und unter,' sondern freilich mit, aber immer über und gegenüber dem menschlichen Tun.") This general statement which Barth made in a discussion on the doctrine of work is a fair description of his general conception of the relationship between God and man.[13] God works "with" human activity, but he does not use it as a means. His work occurs always *über und gegenüber dem menschlichen Tun*. The Bible is something human since it consists of words spoken and written

---

[13] *Die kirchliche Dogmatik* III:4, *op. cit.*, p. 597.

by human persons under historical circumstances. The human element in this word does not become the bearer of a divine activity which operates in the world and continues to perform divine acts until the history of salvation is finished. The human element refers back as a witness to a God who has no enemies or opposition, and who does not need to act any longer to realize his will. He has appeared once, revealed himself in Christ; a God without face who at one point has shown his face.

When Barth speaks of "the word of God in three forms"—proclaimed in preaching, written in the Bible, and "revealed" in Christ—it is important to note that only this last, "the revelation," is really the divine Word. The spoken and the written words are "signs." [14] If we want to meet the divine Word itself, we must go back by way of the spoken and written word to the point where the Word became flesh, which happened in the birth of Jesus. In comparison with this absolute revelation the written and the spoken word appear rather obscure. The activity in the first revelation, in Christ, does not continue through the written and the spoken word. That emphasis is not present in Barth. The reason why the activity does not continue is that it was not really present in the first place, in the incarnation. And the reason that this activity does not determine this first point is that the gospel of Christ needs not crush any power of the law, it simply reveals what the unknown God is like.

Essentially, therefore, revelation is an unwritten word that precedes scripture. This weakens Barth's emphasis that the word is a word to man, a call, a kerygma. The written and spoken word does not appear as an act of God directed toward the hearer. But this means that Barth's conception of the exter-

[14] *Ibid.*, I:1, p. 114 f., and I:2, p. 554 f.

nal word is a part of his total point of view. It is difficult to say what is primary and what is secondary in this connection. Since he does not conceive of God as active, the law cannot be understood as God's activity through which God compels men to work. Instead the law becomes a source from which man can receive knowledge of God's will; and, if the law preceded the gospel, then man would know of God before the gospel. Therefore, the law does not precede the gospel. The question of knowledge dominates the system from the beginning. When the reign of law is not the system against which the gospel contends, the gospel cannot retain its character of an act of God against something. The gospel only unveils what is true being and what is merely appearance. As a gospel of incarnation or "revelation" the gospel is from the beginning conceived of intellectually. Because of this intellectualized point of view there can be no place for the law alongside of the gospel. Everything supports everything else in Barth's theology.

If Barth is permitted to construct his whole system in peace, remove the objective existence of evil, the natural knowledge of God, the rule of law in the world, place the revelation of God through the incarnation in the center, define the gospel as a word about God's disclosure of himself; if he can do all this, then within this framework he can use the whole vocabulary of the New Testament. He can speak of our sin and guilt, our hostility to God, our demonic character. Everything is here, but it is within the frame of reference of our ignorance, and it is a reality only on the basis of our ontological mistake which makes the nonexistent evil into something that exists. Barth has the ability to a very large degree of being able to employ the language of scripture in a system that is totally foreign to the Bible. The point at which this appears most clearly is in his frank and frequent denial of the objective existence of evil. For this reason volume III:3 of *Die kirchliche Dogmatik* (1950), is extremely important for an understanding of his theology.

Finally we must note a very important feature in Barth's recent studies: his tendency to interpret the gospel as law, as a certain political order, or as a definite social program. This is the peculiar way in which the law takes revenge. When it is driven out from its proper and relatively modest place, where it is to be overcome by the gospel, it returns in another form. But now it aspires to enter the holy of holies, to overcome the gospel itself and to make the gospel its servant. Already his book *Rechtfertigung und Recht* appears questionable from this point of view. Here he actually derives common justice, law, and order in the state, out of justification, on the basis of a christological interpretation of Rom. 13:1-7.[15]

Aside from the fact that this exegesis appears absurd, the very need for such an exegesis indicates that something is wrong with the whole system. If justice cannot be derived from the gospel, he evidently finds it difficult to speak of justice at all. This is the starting point. Barth and his followers have come to this point after opposing for years the conception that the law rules over man, and by rejecting the idea of a secular government under which God drives men to be active within their human fellowship in the community. The gospel as a word of God's revelation has been placed over against man's lack of knowledge of God. And now the fact that civil justice exists has become a problem. This justice must now be derived from Christology. But that was merely the beginning. His real ability to derive everything from the

[15] K. Barth, *Rechtfertigung und Recht (Theol. Studien 1)* (2nd ed., 1944), p. 20 ff.

gospel appears more fully in *Christengemeinde und Bürgergemeinde* and in *Die kirchliche Dogmatik* III:2.[16] It is possible that his skill in this respect has not yet reached its highest point.

In this respect Barth differs quite noticeably from Nygren. The law was the critical point also in Nygren's system. In Nygren's work during the 1940 decade the doctrine of the two ages plays a prominent part, and we note there a more positive attitude toward the conception of the law. But the essential is nevertheless the fundamental agreement between this new development and the original conception of the Agape motif. The whole emphasis is on the fact that the new age has come. It is the same overemphasis on "the new man" which appeared in Nygren's work from the beginning. But there is no attempt to derive regulations for society from this new age or from the gospel. That is, however, typical for Barth. There are, to be sure, only "signs," "analogies," "references," etc., and consequently the external rules do not quite assume the character of laws. There is always something temporary and relative in Barth's constructions. But we must not overlook how emphatically he asserts his conception of human fellowship as a doctrine.[17] On the basis of the gospel,

[16] K. Barth, *Christengemeinde und Bürgergemeinde (Theol. Studien 20)* (1946).

[17] *Die kirchliche Dogmatik* III:2, p. 384. "The fundamental assertion of theological anthropology that human existence is an existence in fellowship loses all resemblance to a hypothetical assumption. From this point of view it assumes an axiomatic and dogmatic character. In the Christian church we cannot interpret human nature except as fellowship. And *si quis dixerit hominem esse solitarium, anathema sit.* We may now regard this as demonstrated and proved. For the future history of humanity something may depend on this, whether the Christian church can understand and unite on this, and accept it as established and proved; and thus take this anathema seriously, which so far it has not had the understanding and the courage to do."

democracy, the pattern of life among "the free peoples," appears to him as the necessary social form.[18]

This tendency to incorporate certain external forms of life into the gospel is typical of Barth's more recent works. When the gospel comes to man, it does not stand in tension with any law. The law is not an enemy of the gospel. Instead the law has a tendency to re-appear out of the gospel and act as a friend of the gospel. This law cannot be vanquished by the gospel. The danger inherent in Barth's conception is that the gospel as gospel which bestows, not demands, righteousness loses its essential content. In its place there is a revelation of God in Christ, a revelation which supplies man's lack of knowledge of God; and from this kind of revelation it is possible to derive rules and regulations for human life.

[18] *Christengemeinde und Bürgergemeinde, op. cit.*, p. 36. "Therefore it is not to be overlooked or denied that the Christian, political decisions, judgments, choices, desires, all along the line show a tendency toward the form of the state which, if not realized, yet has been sought and intended in the so-called 'democracies.' When everything is taken into account, we must admit that there is a stronger tendency in this direction than in any other. There is an affinity between the Christian congregation and the society of the free peoples."

CHAPTER SEVEN

Bultmann's Interpretation of the Kerygma

We have several times discussed Bultmann's hermeneutical presuppositions in the chapter on his anthropology, where we tried to define his conception of authentic being (*Dasein*) and his general dependence on Heidegger. In Bultmann it is not only difficult to differentiate between anthropology and hermeneutics: it is impossible. There remain, however, some problems in Bultmann's interpretation of scripture which we have not examined.

In the chapter on "Review and Perspective" we left Bultmann out of consideration and concentrated rather on Nygren and Barth. These two present especially the theological problem of the law, and in that chapter we concentrated our attention on the analysis of the place of law in systematic theology. It is obvious that the question of law is not the only problem in a theological anthropology. It is the avoidance of this problem in modern, systematic literature that justifies us in giving it this prominent place. The task we have assumed is to examine this modern theology critically, not to present our own positive system.

We have indicated that Bultmann's attitude toward the problem of the law differs from that of Barth and Nygren. Bultmann starts with the assumption that man is guilty. His philosophical anthropology permits him to give a positive definition to the concept of guilt even independently of the biblical material. Bultmann is able, therefore, as we have repeatedly

129

pointed out, to emphasize the character of the written and the spoken word as an act (*Tat Gottes*). In this respect he differs from the other two theologians. Yet the specific problem for Bultmann is nevertheless the problem of the law, although in a slightly different form. The program of demythologizing implies that the law is spiritualized. This fact is connected with the process of spiritualization to which the New Testament kerygma is subjected by Bultmann. In this chapter we intend to pay special attention to this feature in Bultmann's theology.

It is appropriate first to review certain characteristic features of Bultmann's point of view and repeat them here. One essential element is the part which "now," the present, plays in his thinking. The question whether something has actually happened in the past in Christ may be completely eliminated. It is not only that it is impossible to find acceptable answers to such a question, but the question as such destroys faith; it kills faith and introduces doubt. To ask such a question is to flee from the decision in which the word of Christ places me now in the present. Or rather, to ask this question means by itself that I have already chosen unreality. It is to seek "security" in objective facts instead of seizing the possibility of new life which is offered to me in the word which I now hear.[1]

If we turn in the other direction, we meet the same attitude on the part of Bultmann. The question whether there will be a resurrection in the future can be eliminated. It is not only impossible to find acceptable answers to such a question, but the question itself destroys faith; it kills faith and introduces

[1] *Glauben und Verstehen, op. cit.,* I, p. 113. "Faith is deed and is secure only in the act of faith itself. To make it a problem for examination afterwards is to deny its reality; it is to seek faith in concrete things rather than in the act. But he who seeks it in tangible things is punished by doubt."

doubt. To ask such a question is to flee from the decision in which the kerygma places me in the present. My future life is offered to me now in the gospel proclaimed to me, and to speak of eternal life apart from this word is to speak of something entirely different. To do so means that we assume the role of a spectator and seek after facts and guarantees in order to make the positive decision after we have found a foundation on which we can rest. But while we search, we make a negative decision. This search in itself is unreality; it means that we have made a choice and turned our back on eternal life. Eternal life meets me at only one single point: in the word which now is proclaimed to me.[2]

In regard to the concept of guilt we have established that a peculiar "egocentricity" dominates Bultmann's thinking on this point. This is due to the influence of Heidegger. Guilt is lack of self-realization, just as salvation is self-realization. Human life (*Dasein*) has fallen, but it has fallen exclusively from itself. When man searches and chooses among the possibilities which meet him in the hour of decision, he is seeking

---

[2] *Ibid.*, p. 37. "But he who would further ask about the necessity, the right and the foundation of faith, receives only one answer in which he is directed to the message of faith which confronts him with a demand to be believed. He receives no answer which at any point justifies his right to faith. Otherwise the word would not be God's word. Then God could be called to account, and faith would not be obedience. The word enters into our world in a manner completely casual, contingent, and as an event. There is no guarantee on the basis of which we may believe. There is no possibility of appealing to someone else, be he Paul or Luther. To us faith can never become a fixed point according to which we direct ourselves, it is always only a new deed, a new obedience. We are always uncertain as soon as we as men look around us and ask; always uncertain as soon as we reflect upon it, or speak about it; certain only in the act. We are always certain only by faith in the forgiving grace of God who justifies us when it pleases him. All our acts and talk are significant only in regard to the grace of forgiveness; and we do not control this, we can only believe it."

his own existence. The New Testament gospel offers man "life," and this means that the gospel offers man that existence which he had lost. Saying "yes" to the word means to receive one's own existence from the word; saying "no" is to reject one's life. There are several elements in Bultmann's presentation which limit and modify the egocentric concentration implied in such a conception of guilt and salvation, but the tendency to make self the center is never completely absent. This is so because the law is spiritualized, and the neighbor and the demands emanating from the neighbor have to yield at decisive points to a philosophical doctrine of "humanity" (*Menschsein*).

Finally, we have noted in Bultmann an inclination to treat the death of Christ and the resurrection of Christ in quite different ways. Both of these are a part of the kerygma. To each one belongs a corresponding, tangible, and observable event. For the death of Christ there is an external event, an observable crucifixion, a person dies. For the resurrection there is also an external event: an observable, audible proclamation that can be heard and also read in the New Testament. Someone proclaims or *preaches* the crucified and risen Lord.

This idea that the resurrection of Christ issues into the apostolic proclamation is very typical of Bultmann's presentation. This interpretation cuts off the long line which in the New Testament combines the resurrection of Christ on the third day with the resurrection of the dead on the last day. In the New Testament preaching joins these two resurrections together. After the resurrection of Christ and the outpouring of the Spirit the proclamation goes out to the ends of the earth, and when it has reached that point, the end comes (Matt. 24:14; Acts 1:6-8; 26:23). The risen Christ is in the gospel and comes to men in preaching. When he reaches them, then they are in his resurrection; then the dead arise, the end has come. In Bultmann's interpretation this long line contracts into one point: the proclamation.[3] The resurrection of Christ lies hidden in the preaching. Our own resurrection which we waited for is hidden there also. And the preaching is now, in the present. Do not look forward or backward in a vain search for security. Just listen! That which you hear is your own existence, your true life; what the New Testament calls simply "life." In this "realized eschatology" of Bultmann with its emphasis on the present the whole program of the dismissal of mythology is an inevitable part. The program of demytholo- gizing had been defined already in *Glauben und Verstehen*, I (1933).[4] It is strange that his essay on "The New Testament and Mythology" (1940) should have occasioned such a great surprise. Everything in this essay was old and familiar.

This concentration on one's own existence, the identification

[3] *Kerygma and Myth, op. cit.,* p. 41. "Christ meets us in the preaching as one crucified and risen. He meets us in the word of preaching and nowhere else. The faith of Easter is just this—faith in the word of preaching.

"It would be wrong at this point to raise again the problem of how this preaching arose historically, as though that could vindicate its truth. That would be to tie our faith in the word of God to the results of historical research. The word of preaching confronts us as the word of God. It is not for us to question its credentials. It is we who are questioned, we who are asked whether we will believe the word or reject it. But in answering this question, in accepting the word of preaching as the word of God and the death and resurrection of Christ as the eschatological event, we are given an opportunity of understanding ourselves. Faith and unbelief are never blind, arbitrary decisions. They offer us the alternative between accepting or rejecting that which alone can illuminate our understanding of ourselves.

"The real Easter faith is faith in the word of preaching which brings illumination. If the event of Easter day is in any sense an historical event additional to the event of the cross, it is nothing else than the rise of faith in the risen Lord, since it was this faith which led to the apostolic preaching."

[4] *Op. cit.,* p. 331, note 2.

of the content of the word of preaching with the hearer's own existence, is made possible because of a peculiarly vague and ambiguous content in the words "death" and "resurrection." The gospel speaks of the death and resurrection of Christ. But, since the gospel must be interpreted existentially or anthropologically, the gospel addressed to me means *my* death and resurrection. Death and resurrection in the gospel are transformed in the preaching into the death and resurrection of the hearer. (The personal name Jesus Christ remains, to be sure. It cannot be interpreted existentially. But this "remnant" is just one of the many indications that there is something radically wrong in Bultmann's whole theory.)

If we now ask what new element is given to the hearer through the gospel, it is practically impossible to find an answer. The reason is that the philosophy of Heidegger, on which Bultmann depends, and which constitutes the basis for his interpretation of the kerygma, already contains a "death and resurrection" in a different form. In my decision I open myself to the future and forsake the past.[5] There is "an old man" in Heidegger's conception of the human being who has fallen from himself; and there is "a new man" in his conception of the true existence to which man opens himself. The anthropology of existentialism is eschatological, a feature which no doubt is derived from Christian sources. It is true, of course, that these philosophers reject and oppose many Christian conceptions. They reject especially all "factualness"; eschatology does not deal with external events, everything is transferred into the existential understanding. It is a dogmatics without God, without Christ, and without eterniy—but a dogmatics nevertheless. What has here been subtracted is found in the New Testament. Now Bultmann takes hold of

[5] *Kerygma and Myth, op. cit.,* p. 28 ff.

the New Testament. Then he demands that its passages shall deal with man; they must be so interpreted that they speak of the experiences of man, not statements about external (historical) events. In consequence the New Testament now contains the anthropology which he had already found in Heidegger. Nothing new can be added. Every part of the argument fits into the general framework.

Even the character of the word as an act, which we have indicated is a specific characteristic of Bultmann's presentation, fits into the proposed scheme. This is true in spite of Bultmann's opinion that at this point he goes beyond what philosophy already asserts.[6] The event of Christ is contained in the word preached in the present. The hearer receives his existence from the word, from "the act of God." He hears himself called to himself. Bultmann therefore returns to this point at the end of his argument when he asks: "Are there still any surviving traces of mythology? There certainly are for those who regard all language about an act of God or of a decisive, eschatological event as mythological."[7] But he does not take the accusation of trafficking in mythology very seriously. From the point of view of the philosophy he employs he does not need to do so. In part he can refer to Kamlah, who expresses himself somewhat ambiguously when he speaks of "a God" who "acts." "Even Kamlah thinks it is philosophically justifiable to use the mythical language of an act of God."[8]

---

[6] *Ibid.*, p. 33. "Here then is the crucial distinction between the New Testament and existentialism, between the Christian faith and the natural understanding of being. The New Testament speaks and faith knows of an act of God through which man becomes capable of self-commitment, capable of faith and love, of his authentic life. . . . Anyone who asserts that to speak of an act of God at all is mythological language is bound to regard this idea of an act of God in Christ as a myth."

[7] *Ibid.*, p. 43.

[8] *Ibid.*, p. 34.

Furthermore—and this is much more important, although Bultmann makes no reference to it—Heidegger himself conceives of conscience in such a way that it becomes the authentic self as a call, a voice crying. Man hears himself called to himself. "Das Dasein ruft im Gewissen sich selbst." [9] Even when Bultmann introduces the concept of the word and begins to speak about "hearing," he is not very far from the philosophical domain to which he belongs.

We must note that according to Heidegger, "being" (*Dasein*) and "existence" are not tangible entities. These do not exist anywhere so that in a moment of illumination it would be possible to see them. It is always a question of possibilities that may be chosen.[10] Consequently man's life is by nature "an ability to become" (*Seinkönnen*) more than it really is.[11] When the conscience calls man to himself, it recalls him (from the point of view of the tangible) to nothing. When man attains to himself, to his real existence, he attains to possibilities. Something new appears, but man himself chooses it. To have life is to have "ability to become," to exist in the present and to have the future which belongs to "ability to become." That something new arises is, therefore, an ordinary human phenomenon. The meaning is not that everything is there, and we gradually discover what is there. Man becomes new in the act of making a choice. This idea of something new is an integral part of this philosophy. When Bultmann speaks of existence coming to man, "hearing" his true existence, etc.,

[9] *Sein und Zeit, op. cit.*, p. 275.
[10] *Ibid.*, p. 42. "Being understands itself always and only in possibilties."
[11] *Ibid.*, p. 145. If we say that it is "more than it is," is implies that we hold a false view of *Dasein* as something tangible. It is more than is "apparent." If we conceive of *Dasein* correctly as ability to become, it is naturally not more than what it is, it is simply what it is. But as "ability to become" it has a future, implied in "ability to *become*." The possibilities are present, too, not only what is apparent.

he continues to move within the confines of his philosophical theory.

The New Testament has not added anything new in principle. There are, on the contrary, indications that the content of the kerygma is the same as the content of Heidegger's conscience. The content of the gospel is the New Testament conception of "life," but this is described exactly as an ability to become: "But just this is life: to have won oneself back as possibility, to be again 'ability to become,' again to have a future." [12] Here the gospel creates a situation identical to that created by the call of conscience. The active character of the proclaimed word is present, but there is also a kind of action in the call of conscience. This call creates a situation in which something new can arise. The gospel does not provide anything more; it gives only an "ability to become" which we possess now in the present, in this moment, nothing else.[13]

We have now reached the point at which we can discuss the critical question which Barth addressed to Bultmann. In how far is this kerygma a gospel? Does it really speak of grace and

[12] *Glauben und Verstehen* I, *op. cit.*, p. 140. "Aber eben dies ist das Leben: sich selbst als Möglichkeit zurückgewinnen, wieder sein im Sein-können, wieder Zukunft haben."

[13] *Ibid.*, p. 147 f. "The character of the new life is now fully clear. Just as the presence of the historic Jesus does not consist in historical effects and reconstructions, and is, therefore, not a tangible reality visible in the present or in the past, but a presence in his authoritative word, so the life is not something visible or tangible, not an intense ardour or experience, but the direction of each present moment by the word, insofar as it is received in faith, and insofar as each present moment is understood as the new possibility of my life as possessing an ability to become, a future."

Ibid., p. 145. "Rather, human life has regained its authentic being in the ability to become; as long as life lasts, it is always an ability to become, and therefore always a new decision, never available, only a future. The life is never a possession, it must be chosen again and again. Therefore every 'now' of this word, 'the word became flesh' is always present in the 'now' of the proclamation, in the moment."

justification? Is it anything else than law, claim, demand? [14]
That which should happen, to which the word calls me, is
nevertheless continually my own decisions, my own choices.
Since the gospel acts in the same way as conscience, the only
difference is that the gospel is a word proclaimed in the church,
while conscience is free from the external form of the sermon.
But that difference is superficial, and it tends to increase the
legalistic aspect of the argument. Churchly legalism has less
of the gospel than any other legalism. It is quite apparent
that Barth's question strikes the weakest point in the program
of demythologizing.

Whether Barth himself preserves the gospel in his theology
is not a pertinent question here. We are now concerned exclusively with Bultmann. We must then affirm that the evangelical character of the word, that the word bestows righteousness, gives and creates life, is something which necessarily
disappears as soon as that which is unique in Christ is lost. It is
significant that the kerygma continually speaks of this one
person, this man by the name Jesus Christ, who is the One
proclaimed to all the others. The fact that the personal name
is left out and cannot be existentially interpreted indicates that
the whole program of the existential interpretation is a mistake.
To preach means to proclaim that something has happened in
Christ once and for all. If we surrender this fact, then we
surrender the kerygma, and then there is no more preaching.
What has happened implies that it has happened for the world,
and therefore the proclamation is to go out into the world.
Preaching and world mission are identical. The death and resurrection of Christ happened in order that the death and
resurrection should go out into the world and take place anew
in the man who hears. This is the good intention in Bultmann's

[14] K. Barth, *Rudolf Bultmann* (1952) p. 18 ff.

theology. But the foundation of this repeated event in person after person is the unique event of Jesus Christ.

Unless the gospel speaks of something that has happened, it is not possible to retain the gospel's sentence of justification which makes the forgiveness of sin a gift rather than something which the hearer accomplishes by his own decisions. When the concrete event is lost, the conception of a gift in the word is also lost. Then the purpose of the word is that something ought to be, something ought to happen. In that case the word makes an appeal to the hearer's ability to act and urges activity (as conscience does). It is not merely a coincidence that the New Testament combines justification with the resurrection of Christ (Rom. 4:25), and that preaching is "in vain" if Christ has not been raised (I Cor. 15:14). That the old man dies and a new, righteous man arises in us rests on something that occurred once for all, the death and resurrection of Christ. If we are to express clearly the character of the proclaimed word as a word of grace, we cannot be indifferent to the question of whether the resurrection of Christ really occurred. The more we empty the word of "what has happened," the more clearly it assumes the character of challenge and demand rather than gospel.

It is necessary to discuss more fully the problem of "historicity" and to define the relation between law and gospel, on the one hand, and the external or the body, on the other hand. It will then become apparent that the vulnerable point in Bultmann's theology, too, is the doctrine of the *law*. When the law becomes spiritualized, the gospel also becomes spiritualized, and the reality of any future event is lost.[15] There is

---

[15] The future must be comprehended in the present when the gospel no longer has anything to say about the body. It is "the giving of life to the mortal body" which is the unique, future element in the New

an intimate connection between law and gospel, on the one hand, and death and resurrection, on the other. If the connection between the word and the external (body) is severed at one point, the connection is broken at other points likewise.

The weakness of the modern theological conception of the law, as we have seen, is that the law is commonly derived from the gospel. The law declares how we should act, and it is assumed that such pronouncements can be made only on the basis of faith, or on the basis of personal choice. In this way the law loses its character as governing authority, and it becomes difficult to see how the power of the law can rest on humanity regardless of the fact whether men believe in it or not. Nevertheless this is the biblical presupposition. The law has this character of pressure and compulsion from which no one escapes.

The best way to understand this biblical conception is to start with the actual demands of community living which every one is able to see. These demands are actually there, because they proceed from other men; and this means that the neighbor is present in them. The neighbor is not an idea that has to be added after the gospel comes. There are, of course, many actual demands which the gospel, when it enters the picture, must deny, but that is perfectly natural. Even Luther held that the secular government misused its power; which

Testament (Rom. 8:11). That the expectation in regard to the body disappears is connected with the fact that the body is not considered as now standing under the law. We have lost the ability to interpret life in this world in all its earthiness; from the point of view that we must labor, wear out, grow old, and die. In respect to these facts both preaching and theology have been silent in these centuries of spiritualization. After such a spiritualization has taken place, it influences the question of the historicity of the resurrection of Christ. We are not able to notice that the proclamation is curtailed when the historicity is rejected. That is perfectly natural, because the curtailment had already been made in the spiritualization of the law.

implies that the government stands under the criticism of the word, although it nevertheless is *God's* government. The more the demands are understood as elementary demands connected with the needs for food, clothing, shelter, etc., the more clearly appears their connection with the biblical view of God's government of the world and with the doctrine of creation. These demands cannot be derived from faith. They are simply there in the social pressures which originate in the needs of others. It is one of the essential characteristics that they come to us from the outside.

This aspect of existence has not been made an object of reflection during the past centuries when theology and philosophy have discussed morality and ethics. We have first removed this area of life, and then we have tried to define the ethical problem. This implies that we have removed the law. We have rejected the biblical doctrine of creation, and in doing so also removed the law.

This is the spiritualization of the law. The law comes from within, from the individual himself who is independent and makes his own laws. If the individual does not choose to make his own law, then there is for the moment no law over him. Then the law becomes an aspect which I apply to my life in the world, and which is not there when I do not apply it. This conception negates the fact that God has created the world and governs it. In consequence of the acceptance of such a conception of the law a large and significant segment of the content of the Christian faith is removed and cannot later be inserted into the presentation. The biblical conception of the law flows directly from the doctrine of creation. The law is simply God's creative will as it appears now in conflict with sin. The law is the correlative of sin. Since sin in me is "the old man," the work of the law is "to put to death," "to crucify," etc. (All of which are expressions taken from the New Testament kerygma of the death and resurrection of Christ.) This work belongs to the law as long as sin remains.

This means that the power of the law ceases only at the last judgment and the resurrection of the dead. The eternal life which then will be given is bestowed now in the word, in the kerygma which proclaims that the death and resurrection of Christ has taken place. The gospel is a gospel because it declares that this has happened. When that has taken place, the end of our own chastening is life, provided we are in Christ by faith.

At every point there is a connection between the word and the external (body). The law governs the whole man. We read of the resurrection of Christ on the third day in the gospels, and to remove the bodily element from this resurrection is possible only on the basis that the bodily element has been removed at every other point. This has generally happened in modern theology. The historicity of the resurrection is eliminated when there are theological reasons for doing so. But these theological reasons are generally untenable and due to a confused reasoning. The general assumption is always the same; if we take away the resurrection on the third day, it becomes significant (and less offensive) to speak of the forgiveness of sin and salvation through Christ. But the real truth is rather that every form of the preaching of Christ and every assertion that something is given "through him" presupposes that Christ is the One and Only; a presupposition that is just as offensive wherever it appears.

It is just as impossible to speak of forgiveness in Christ as to talk about resurrection in Christ. There is the same kind of improbability in the resurrection and in the forgiveness of sin. In principle the difficulty is the same. If we may use Bultmann's terminology, we could say: the preaching of Christ is as such mythology. The proper name, Jesus Christ, is never assimilated in the existential interpretation. It is inconsistent to remove mythology and still retain the kerygma. Here we have come to the chief point. If we start with the gospel and assume that it is the task of theology to interpret the gospel, we must ask the important question: How can the gospel remain a gospel if it does not proclaim something that has happened, or tell of events that have actually taken place? The answer to that question is simple and unequivocal. The gospel is by its very nature a message about events that have taken place, and to remove this aspect of it is to remove the gospel.

These arguments have been presented in one of my earlier books, but then in opposition to the Lundensian theology represented by A. Nygren and R. Bring.[16] The kerygma speaks about events. Therefore it does not fit into the Lundensian distinction between "religious" and "theoretical" propositions. The kerygmatic assertions become somewhat "theoretical" when examined from the point of view of Nygren's critical philosophy. We have already shown that Nygren's method is not adequate for a correct interpretation of the New Testament. There is no reason to regard the kerygmatic assertion as dubious just because it says that the resurrection has taken place and regards this as true. There is, on the contrary, good reason to cease using the contrast, "religious—theoretical," if we desire to give an historically accurate description of the biblical material. It is, of course, faith which says that the resurrection has occurred. That is stated also in *Predikan*. "It should also be pointed out that we have never intended to present the resurrection as a plausible event. Our thesis is a

[16] G. Wingren, *Predikan* (*Preaching*) (Lund, 1949).

different one: the Christian faith believes that it is true that Christ rose from the dead. If this fundamental fact is given up, faith is destroyed. We should not talk about faith apart from this. But this which faith says is true is just as incredible as that God forgives sins." [17] Faith comes from preaching, and preaching proclaims both. It proclaims the resurrection of Christ and thereby also the forgiveness of sin. Both are received from the word, which is a word of grace, a gift, not a demand.

The argument presented in *Predikan* may be applied without change to Bultmann's program of demythologizing. The kerygma speaks of definite events. The death and the resurrection of Christ stand in the center. Now when the death and resurrection are to be interpreted existentially, the meaning of the kerygma becomes the same as the call of conscience. Bultmann tries, of course, to retain justification as the content of the kerygma, while removing the resurrection as an actual event. He wants to interpret death differently from sin. Sin is not a mythological conception; and, therefore, "forgiveness" as an "act of God" is not a mythological concept.[18]

But the idea that death rules over man is mythological, and the resurrection as a liberation from the power of death becomes, therefore, an untenable element in the kerygma. But this is an impossible separation between sin and death, forgiveness and resurrection. To realize one's bondage under death is possible only by a leap into the kerygma. But anyone who conceives of himself as under bondage to sin has already made a leap into the kerygma. "Mythology" begins much sooner than Bultmann realizes. It begins when One, individually named, is proclaimed to the others as hearers. The funda-

[17] *Ibid.*, p. 182, n. 37.
[18] *Kerygma and Myth, op. cit.*, p. 31.

mental offense is that the kerygma deals with only one person and preaches about this One to all the rest. This fundamental offense does not become greater by asserting that this One rose from the dead on the third day.

We must now return to the problem of the spiritualization of the law to which we have already called attention. This problem is connected with a very strange element in Bultmann's position. He regularly accuses his critics of confusing *existentiell* and *existential*.[19] It is not easy, however, to avoid this mistake if we are to consider Bultmann at all. Bultmann himself continually and consistently confuses *existentiell* and *existential*. The decisive point is that he combines two subjects in an intimate relationship: preaching and the existentialist analysis of Being. If the sermon is to have any meaning at all, it should be related to man's existential decisions. If that were really done, the spiritualization of the law could be avoided within Bultmann's system. In that case the kerygma would be associated with the hearer's everyday life. But now that the sermon is connected with the exisentialist analysis, the spiritualization of the law becomes inevitable.

When Bultmann criticizes Martin Dibelius' book on historical and super-historical religion in Christianity, he also discusses the conception of neighbor in the New Testament.[20] He contends that if we conceive of the man of faith as belonging to a super-temporal existence, he really has no actual neighbors but only certain beings surrounding him on whom he can pour

[19] Up to this point it has not been necessary in translation to differentiate between these two terms. Reginald H. Fuller in *Kerygma and Myth* defines *existentiell* as "that which belongs to existence as such," and *existential* as "that which belongs to the particular philosophical system called existentialism." He uses "existential" for the former and "existentialist" for the latter. (*Kerygma and Myth, op. cit.,* p. xi.).

[20] *Glauben und Verstehen, op. cit.,* I, 80.

out the powers of his new life. In correcting Dibelius he then presents his own conception. "But the neighbor is the one with whom I am continually connected in my own concrete historical being. The concept of neighbor depends on a conception of human life as fellowship, which limits my own existence, and without which 'man' would be an abstraction. If the real man exists in this fellowship, he has a real historical existence with its concrete historical demands." [21]

This conception, too, has its source in Heidegger. One of the most original features of Heidegger's analysis of "being" is that man is defined in his "everyday" life. He never exists alone, he is in the world, busy with things in the world and associating with other men. These others are not impersonal beings found here and there. We meet them "in work," in their strivings, in their life in the world. Here we are close to insights which were fundamental for the development of the Lutheran doctrine of the call. These very associations with others mean that I am confronted with demands originating in them. On the basis of this element, which appears momentarily in Heidegger and Bultmann, the egocentric tendency in both systems, the concentration on *my* existence, could have been limited.

But this does not happen. Here it is impossible to discuss the reasons for this failure. In this connection we direct our attention to this one feature: that Bultmann does not regard preaching, the proclamation of the biblical word, as addressed directly to concrete historical situations. That was done in the Reformation, and it gave to its preaching an element of concrete reality. But Bultmann's interest is directed toward the purely formal, philosophical analysis of all human existence. The result of this formal analysis is immediately and directly

[21] *Ibid.*, p. 81.

associated with a factor which is not at all congruent with it, viz., preaching, the call of the word to men who live in the concrete decisions and difficulties of the world. In his approach Bultmann methodically mixes preaching and theology together. Theology is to carry out the program of demythologizing, but the object that is demythologized is the present Christian proclamation.[22] Mythology must be removed from preaching. And the criterion for this process is the existentialist analysis of Being. Bultmann's procedure at this point is simply an example of his general tendency to confuse theology and preaching. From the point of view of the church the general criticism of Bultmann has been that the objective reality of the New Testament miracles disappears out of preaching. But there is another side of the program which ought to receive just as much attention: the positive task of establishing a connection between the word of preaching and the hearer's concrete everyday life with its existential decisions is completely left out of consideration.

This is what we mean by the statement that the law is spiritualized. Guilt is separated from the relationship to the neighbor and is given an egocentric character: I have not realized my own existence. At the same time the gospel becomes egocentric; it gives me my existence, my life as "an ability to become" (*Seinkönnen*). On the basis of Bultmann's premises we could have expected an entirely different program for

[22] *Kerygma and Myth, op. cit.,* p. 3. "We are therefore bound to ask whether, when we preach the gospel today, we expect our converts to accept not only the gospel message, but also the mythical view of the world in which it is set. If not, does the New Testament embody a truth which is quite independent of its mythical setting? If it does, theology must undertake the task of stripping the Kerygma from its mythical framework, of 'demythologizing' it." This general program is not changed by what Bultmann says in *Kerygma und Mythos,* II, 201-203. In his criticism of preaching he maintains the same negative attitude.

the sermon. We could have expected a combination of an existentialist sermon with men's existentialist decisions. The program of demythologizing could have been carried out anyway without making it the principal task, without this passionate emphasis on the *de*, on the minus sign, the subtraction. The preacher could then have assumed the concrete entanglements in the relationship to the neighbor, and in that sense a rule of law. The idea of guilt would then have had a different content. The gospel would not be concerned simply with the individual and his existence.

But Bultmann does not do this, and the reason is that he objectifies Heidegger's philosophy as a universal, scientific doctrine of "man's being," and uses this doctrine as a norm for actual contemporary preaching. The only error in preaching which can be demonstrated under such a norm is the presence of tangible and corporeal (mythical) conceptions. That the sermon is abstract, without contact with the actual life of the hearers, is an error which escapes his analysis. Bultmann's program contributes rather toward making modern preaching even more abstract, separated from actual life and devoted to the spiritualized conception of the law. The program of spiritualization affects the whole system.

Beyond doubt Bultmann consciously strives toward this general spiritualization. But it is important to detect the connection between this spiritualization of the law and the disappearance of the future in the interest of an eschatology in the present, as well as the transformation of the resurrection of Christ into a preaching about the resurrection. There is an inner unity in these various factors. Bultmann's problem, too, is in reality the problem of the law.

Finally we must add one more observation. If we desire to separate theology and preaching, we do not thereby accept

Nygren's separation of "the theoretical" and "the religious." The kerygma is something else than theology, but the point of difference is not what Nygren assumes. Nygren holds that the question of truth is the specific question in the theoretical context. The question of truth is, therefore, shut out from the three other non-theoretical contexts of meaning. It is inevitable, therefore, to regard these as productive forms of life. It is more reasonable not to use the term "truth" when we try to indicate something "specific" in a certain area. The scientist naturally asks about truth, but what is specific for science is that the scientific investigator guards against personal involvements and strives for pure objectivity.

The biblical writers follow the opposite course. They speak about realities, but the speaker is not, and cannot be, separated from these realities. This is true also in the direct proclamation of the word. The speaker and the hearer are both in principle involved in the kerygma. If we remove the speaker and the hearer, we remove the kerygma. But this involvement in the word does not mean that the question about truth is immaterial. The kerygma is in principle a word about events that have happened, and these events are historical events in which the corporeal and the earthly participate. The preaching proclaims something that has happened. Its character as gospel and gift depends on the fact that what is proclaimed has actually happened. The question about the truth is vital to the kerygma. If we describe faith as indifferent to knowledge (in this sense), we misrepresent faith. To deny the truth of the resurrection narrative in the common and ordinary sense implies a denial of the gospel.

CHAPTER EIGHT

Retrospect and Conclusion

In our presentation we have made three individual theologians the object of our study. To summarize what we have said about these three in the course of our analysis would be simply a repetition of the results. Insofar as the presentation has dealt with these three individuals we regard it as complete.

During our examination certain fundamental points of view have been established. These scattered viewpoints do not enable us to present our own positive definition of a theological method. Casual in nature, they have been discovered in the negative context of our criticism of contemporary systematic literature. But it may be proper to review them, summarize, and broaden them a little further.

First of all it would be helpful to examine what possibilities our presentation has given us to express ourselves constructively. We have consistently made a selection of the problems and of the criteria applied to the solution of those problems offered by contemporary theologians. This procedure imposes a limitation on us as we begin this chapter, and it may clarify matters to state what those limitations are.

In the first place, we have elected to make anthropology and hermeneutics the exclusive object of our examination. We have temporarily ignored any other problems. This implies that two definite problems have been isolated from all the other problems.

In the second place, we have chosen to test the contemporary theological attitude to anthropological and hermeneutical questions on the basis of one single criterion. We have asked only one question: Are the anthropological and hermeneutical presuppositions tenable on the basis of scripture? In the Introduction we stated explicitly that other points of view could very well be used in evaluating the modern theological production.

In the third place, we have made a definite selection within the area of anthropology. In the chapter on "Review and Perspective," which closed the discussion on anthropology, we confined ourselves to one single point: the doctrine of the law. The question about the law is certainly not the only anthropological problem. We decided to concentrate our attention on it because the study of contemporary theology forces us to consider this special area.

In the fourth place, this concentration on the law had some definite consequences for our approach to the hermeneutical problem. We have emphasized that the gospel in the New Testament implies a liberation from bondage, and that it is questionable whether this aspect of the gospel appears clearly in modern theology. This bondage is not exclusively a bondage under law and guilt, although we have paid special attention to this one point. In this case, too, we have made a selection of problems. Hermeneutics does not deal only with the relationship between law and gospel. We have, however, concentrated attention on this extremely important relationship which cannot be ignored in any correct interpretation of the scriptures. Even in this area it is the study of contemporary, systematic literature that has compelled our presentation to assume this form.

Finally, in the fifth place, the choice of these three theologians has compelled us to be selective, isolating certain points

151

of view, concentrating on some aspects and omitting others. This is the chief reason for the limitations that have been imposed on this study. There are many theologians at work in the modern world, but we have selected these three: Nygren, Barth, and Bultmann. As a consequence this study assumes the character of a provisional work, at least from a positive and methodological point of view. But even such a book may have something to say that is relevant for the general problem of the theological method. We have noted the limitations, but we may also point out some positive results.

In our presentation we have assumed that systematic theology cannot confine itself to historical problems of the type dealt with in church history. The question of whether history of dogma or history of thought belong in the department of systematics or in church history receives a different answer in different countries. On the continent history of dogma generally is listed under church history; in Sweden, however, it belongs to the department of systematics. When a Swedish theologian examines continental, systematic theology, he must not expect the systematic theologian to deal with purely historical problems. That would be an unfair demand. But he may certainly expect that, if the continental theologian in solving his purely systematic problems expresses himself on some historical matters, as he may be compelled to do, then these statements ought to be correct.

This same demand must be made in regard to Swedish theology.[1] In this theology the historical problems occupy a central place. In fact, every statement made by a systematic

---

[1] The criticism we have directed against Nygren, Barth, and Bultmann is in all these instances an historical criticism. It is important to keep this in mind, especially in regard to Lundensian theology. This theology is not correct historically and weak in systematics, but it is wrong in its historical approach.

theologian who uses the method of motif research is a statement about historical relationships. But it is important to underscore that Nygren's motif research is specifically designed to solve the systematic problem. He proposes to solve that problem by historical study because his philosophy of religion compels him to try just that solution. The questions are formal, the answers are found in history. Whoever is going to solve the systematic problem, i.e., discover the answer to the question of the uniqueness of the Christian faith, has to examine the historical material. But it is the systematic problem that is to be solved by this method.

Nygren emphasizes that motif research is not a purely historical study. Even though this method deals with historical material, it is "a specific method of systematic theology, although it is carried through within given historical material. If motif research succeeds in establishing the fundamental Christian motif, the problem of systematic theology is then in principle solved, because the answer is then given to the question of the uniqueness of the Christian faith. This is the chief question for systematic theology. What work it has beyond this is simply to develop what is already given in this fundamental motif." [2] An example of this method is given when the results of the study of Luther are used to answer the question: What is Christianity? This procedure is typical of Swedish theology.

In discussing the authentic, systematic problem, it may be helpful to state this positive thesis: The historical and systematic disciplines have two different functions which cannot be interchanged. The direct use of the results of Luther research in systematics indicates lack of both systematic and historical insight. This procedure ignores the fact that Luther's

[2] *Philosophy and Motif Research, op. cit.*, p. 89.

theology is localized in the sixteenth century, and that his interpretation is bound to that situation. Whoever pursues this method fails to realize that the systematic problem, as a problem of what the Christian faith means now, in the present, cannot be solved by materials gathered from Luther's writings. This problem remains unsolved. In fact, motif research prevents this problem from being properly presented.

This lack of understanding depends on two factors. In the first place, Luther interprets the law in the categories of the sixteenth century, and his interpretation is bound to that situation. That was the proper way of interpreting the gospel in the sixteenth century, and the Reformers accepted that as their task. All good interpretation of the Bible is contemporary. If it were not so, it would not be good. In that case the gospel would not encounter the actual, enslaving law. Since Lundensian theology does not operate with an interpretation of the law, but uses the purely formal Agape-motif, it is not able to see how every interpretation of scripture is tied in with the contemporary situation. It can, therefore, take the material from Luther out of its context into the twentieth century and make it furnish a solution to a systematic problem.

In the second place, the New Testament and the Reformation regard the gospel as a word addressed to man; a word that is to be proclaimed and preached. The Reformation proceeds as a proclamation of the gospel over against the law. Since Lundensian theology does not conceive of the gospel as a spoken word, it cannot understand the biblical material as a word which functions in every period of time. The New Testament material becomes "religious propositions" in the first century; Luther's writings become "religious propositions" in the sixteenth century; and the "religious propositions" of the twentieth century cannot be enunciated by scientific theology. When they are spoken, they will become the object of motif research in the future.

But from a strictly historical point of view this is a mistake. Luther's theology is interpretation of the Bible. All theology of the past is such interpretation. The Bible is not on a par with the subsequent interpretation; it is above it, as the text is antecedent to the commentary. And the interpretation is always an interpretation for the time in which it is writen or spoken. Since we must solve both historical and systematic problems in the discipline of systematic theology, it is necessary to keep these strictly separated. A study of the writings from the sixteenth century does not by itself solve any contemporary, systematic problems. It solves historical problems. These historical problems need to be solved, but they are solved more easily if the historical material is not expected to furnish solutions to our contemporary problems. Then we also see clearly that the question of the significance of the Bible for our time remains unsolved even after the historical problem has been solved.

Our second positive thesis also concerns a separation, and here we can resume our criticism of Bultmann. It will then become clear what we mean by the assertion that the biblical word functions in every period of time, and that it always appears connected with the contemporary situation. When Bultmann makes contemporary preaching the object of demythologizing, he co-ordinates the sermon and the *existentialist,* philosophical analysis of being. On the basis of Bultmann's own starting point we might have expected a different, positive conception of preaching: a co-ordination of preaching with man's *existential* decisions. Preaching is the word of the Bible addressed to people who live in the concrete decisions and difficulties in the world. This program would have implied a radical separation between the sermon and scientific theology. Theology and philosophy would then have been left out for the present. The kerygma would have been conceived of as functioning apart from all scientific concerns, as the scriptural word addressed to men in their everyday life. It would then have been impossible to separate the kerygma from these concrete situations; and, therefore, the kerygma would not have become abstract and spiritualized. The gospel would then function in the realm where the law also functions.

The meaning of this will become clearer if we use a different terminology, independently of our criticism of Bultmann's program of demythologizing. We have already suggested a separation between theology and history. Now we propose to distinguish between theology and preaching. Looking back over the history of Christian thought, we see that it is a history of a continuous interpretation of the Bible century after century. The same texts are continually interpreted. The word of the Bible does not reside back in its own century to be succeeded by "religious statements" in subsequent times. The word of the Bible itself is repeated and spoken to each succeeding generation. An historian who treats these interpretations as relative understands them correctly. The interpretation is always somewhat removed from the Bible; it contains mistakes and misunderstandings. These interpretations of the past are also removed from our present situation. They do not answer our questions. As historians we recognize that all previous interpretations are bound to their own environment. This is obvious. But now we are also concerned with the question of the interpretation produced now in the present.

It is generally assumed that this contemporary interpretation is the task of systematic theology. This is a mistake. Theology simply has to proceed on the assumption that interpretation continues. It is actually going on now in our time in the preaching and the teaching which take place within the now existing Christian congregations. There the interpretation of scripture has its rightful place. The kerygma can remain a kerygma only in these situations in the church. There it is a word from which the hearer cannot be separated. In scientific study the scholar and the person addressed must be detached from the subject. Scientific theology stands on the sidelines and observes as the actual preaching now takes place.

Science depends on objective reasoning in the sense that it does not deal with anything which cannot be observed and understood by any one person. If the sermon engages in arguments in this sense, it ceases to be a sermon. The sermon brings forth the gospel, and the gospel bestows something on man which he does not possess independently of the gospel, and which is obtainable only by faith in the gospel. The agency for the interpretation of the word, therefore, is not scientific theology, but the sermon, including teaching, administration of the sacraments, pastoral care, etc.

If we see a musical composition on paper, we do not associate these notes primarily with the science of musical theory. The intention expressed in these notes is that the composition should be played or sung. If we attend a concert where the paper with the notes lies on the music rack, we witness a performance that voluntarily is subjected to the score. We observe the several parts of the action, both the original composition and the actual playing. We can criticize the presentation objectively without thereby taking part in the performance.

The same situation obtains in regard to a code of law. The code is promulgated in order that the court may have an objective standard. If we now enter the courtroom, we witness a performance taking place according to the legal code; but this action is not a scientific legal study. The science of jurisprudence stands aside and observes how actual judgments are pronounced according to definite laws.

The same relationship which obtains between the composition and the performance, and between the law and the court action, obtains also between the text of the Bible and the sermon delivered now in the present. The nature of the sermon is such that it is subordinated to the text which is read and expounded. The theologian does not himself become a preacher if he assumes that this is the meaning of the sermon; just as the scientific student of law does not become a judge because he holds that in the courts a decision is rendered according to the law; or, just as the music critic does not become a performer by assuming that the composition announced is the one that was to be played at the concert. The claim that the word of the Bible is spoken in our time and to the men of today is already made in the simple fact that preaching is now going on. Scientific theology does not raise this claim. It simply observes that the claim has been made. And it has before itself both the original text, the biblical writings (the composition), and the continuous, observable, readable, and audible exposition of the text (the actual playing of the composition).

Parenthetically it may be necessary to anticipate an objection at this point. It might be claimed that not everything in the Bible is kerygma. Some of it is instruction, *didache*, or something else. That is true. But from the general point of view suggested above this objection carries no weight. If the text is *didache*, it should be used in teaching. If it is a cultic text, it should be used in the cult. There is very likely no part of the Bible which is not intended to be used in one way or another in a practical situation. If we now consider the present "use" of the biblical material, we find such use along the whole line. It appears most clearly in the sermon, which claims to be simply the means whereby the biblical word speaks now in the present. But in principle we find that the same things occur at every point in the activity which now takes place in the Christian congregation: teaching, worship, confession, etc. The original word is spoken now to our generation. Theology observes this whole phenomenon critically. It has no other function than to examine it on the basis of the claim raised by the phenomenon itself.

Barth used this phenomenological approach in the first volume of his dogmatics. "Es predigt in der Welt, so gewiss und so wahrnehmbar, als es regnet." [3] He combined a purely phenomenological approach with an existential-philosophical one. But later on, in *Die kirchliche Dogmatik* (1932), both of these approaches were abandoned. Dogmatics was placed *in* the church and regarded as a function of the church. It is difficult for Barth to see any other possibilities. The reason for this is that he has removed the law as a power that rules over man even before the preaching of the gospel appears. But if we refuse to make this Barthian mistake, we can start with a twofold, purely phenomenological approach.

At the close of our discussion of the anthropological presuppositions we observed the methodological difficulties which confront systematic theology because modern, philosophical thinking does not recognize any rules of conduct as "right" or tenable from a theoretical point of view. This situation has forced theology to recognize an ethos which can somehow be derived from the Christian faith. When we observe the Christian faith, we find implicit in this faith an ethos which can

[3] *Die christliche Dogmatik, op. cit.,* I, 32.

become the object of description and analysis. At first sight this idea might seem very acceptable, and it has also been widely adopted. But even from a purely descriptive point of view we have found that this is a misleading argument which results in a perverted interpretation of historical situations. The preaching of the gospel presupposes an already existing realm of law. A description based on this modern, philosophical approach becomes a different type of ethos from that contained in the historical material of primitive Christianity and the Reformation. We cannot derive the law from the Christian faith when the gospel on which the faith is based presupposes a law which rules even before the gospel. This method of derivation corrupts the gospel material, and cannot, therefore, be a description of it.

It is, of course, true that theology cannot make the assertion that God's law rules the whole world. In science we do not refer to any other arguments than those which everyone can observe and understand. If we have resort to other arguments, we *eo ipso* depart from scientific argumentation and take up some other form of communication; as, for instance, the sermon, which is a form of address. In this situation we found it necessary to start with the actual demand. We do not claim anything more for these demands than that they actually proceed from human, community life.

We recognized, however, that even this simple starting point contains presuppositions foreign to the material, which must later be corrected as the investigation proceeds. Very likely all presuppositions contain elements which make it difficult to observe correctly what actually is contained in the text we read. If this is true of other sciences, it is not very plausible that theology is an exception, or that its scientific character could be established by a methodological program developed before the encounter with the texts. It is naive to expect that the relationship between scientific study and the texts should be free from problems. The very opposite should be expected.

We also assumed that these "demands in human community life" would include ethical points of view, i.e., theories which flourish in the general culture of the time and determine men's conceptions and actions. It is onesided to regard these only from the points of view of whether they are scientifically tenable, or whether they agree with the New Testament conception. We may consider these theories themselves as a power, as a limiting and compelling pressure in human community life.

This was the preliminary result in our chapter on "Review and Perspective." Now in this chapter we conclude that our theology observes the actual, contemporary interpretation of scripture. Our starting point is the observation of two functions: the actual demands (including points of view, theories, etc.), and the actual proclamation (which claims that the original word of scripture is now being spoken in this given situation with its points of view, theories, community structure, etc.). This provides a twofold, purely phenomenological approach.

We do not posit beforehand an abstract doctrine of Being (*Menschsein*). We do not define beforehand any formal, philosophical questions to which the material is supposed to give an answer. These factors which we observe, and to which the whole argument is related, are historical factors, with the only difference that they appear in the present. They are available for observation and study independently of any personal attitude toward them. We would, of course, have to undertake an interpretation of the gospel, an interpretation that can be opposed by another interpretation. But the controversy in such a program of interpretation is connected with concrete,

161

historical material on the basis of which everyone can argue. We would have to undertake an interpretation of prevalent points of view and conventional standards of conduct, an interpretation also open for discussion. But the possibility of a purely factual argumentation is constantly present.

At no point do we refer to anything which cannot be observed and understood by everyone. It is not demanded that theology should be based on existential philosophy; nor is theology a discipline of the church. The approach is purely phenomenological. We observe certain operating functions, and we do not apply external norms to these functions. We simply note that one of these functions, the sermon, has itself assumed a norm for itself. It makes the claim that it is now, in this situation, an interpretation of the gospel—this definite message which is contained in well-defined texts.

One objection may properly be raised against this conception of the theological program. The subjects under consideration are so extensive and varied that it would be impossible to make a total survey and comparison. The undertaking would be scholarly and desirable, but whatever would be said as a result would be approximate and vague. It would be better to forego all scientific discussion on this subject, and let the confrontation take place "on the field" where Christian faith and modern social life meet. The situation is further complicated by the fact that the proclamation of the gospel is always intimately connected with the contemporary scene.

We must recognize this objection as a valid one. In general, theological mistakes and the "isms" arise because we desire to meet this objection by claiming for systematic theology an exactness which it can never attain. It is easy to find "a method" which enables us to produce a lot of books, but which is so easily workable just because it helps us to skip over the really difficult problems instead of solving them. If systematic theology is to make any contribution to general knowledge, it must not ignore the difficulties. If it tries to conceal these difficulties and accept cheap solutions, it will become the prey of temporary fashions from time to time. It should be noted especially in this connection that a concentration on the history of ideas and the neglect of the proper systematic task do not provide a greater degree of exactness.

The research into the history of thought which systematic theology undertakes should provide a total evaluation of given types of interpretation of scripture, evaluate them in the total perspective of the whole, and evaluate them even though they are separated from one another by centuries. When we study a certain event in the life of the church and search for the causes, we are dealing with church history. If we undertake an historical investigation of the biblical documents and their significance at the time of writing, we are working in the discipline of exegesis.

The special task which confronts systematic theology both in its historical and strictly systematic functions is to answer the question: What is the essence of Christianity? In how far is it Platonic, or based on the New Testament? Is the biblical material clearly expressed in this interpretation, or is it suppressed by content derived from other sources? Unless there are questions of this kind, it is meaningless to add another historical discipline to church history and exegesis. The purely individual analysis of the conceptions of certain important people, without comparisons and evaluation, are always undertaken on the basis of a judgment concerning the total development of Christian thought. Without this judgment the individual analyses would lack any scholarly significance.

This judgment, or assumption, regarding the total development, contains a latent systematic theology. The Reformation has been evaluated on the basis of the New Testament, which is 1500 years older; or a comparison has been made between ancient culture and the Renaissance, etc. But this cannot be done without giving up the demand for exact results. We have to ask rather whether it is proper to leave this problem of extensive evaluation out of consideration just because it is possible to work with greater exactness in other sciences which do not present these general problems. In that case we would have to give up a great many scholarly investigations—not only within theology. But these problems would then simply be raised within other areas of research, and become disturbing elements. It is impossible to avoid these problems of total evaluation.

We have insisted on a separation between the historical and the specific systematic function within systematic theology. These are two separate functions. But we must also insist that there is a close relationship between them. In his study of the history of thought the systematic theologian is continually confronted with the interpretations of scripture which belong to various periods and bear the marks of the time in which they originated. These are the only possible kinds of interpretation of the kerygma, since it is always addressed to the contemporary world. But these interpretations must be critically examined on the basis of the word of scripture which they claim to expound, and which remains as an independent factor available for examination apart from these various interpretations. As a systematic theologian in a more restricted sense he confronts the interpretation produced in the present, which in principle must be evaluated in the same way.

It will then become clear that we can understand the various types (types of piety, preaching, organization, etc.) only in the light of history. They have all originated in definite historical situations, which explain much of their structure. But this does not mean that it is unreasonable to subject them to critical analysis. As far as they now exist, they all claim to expound the original word of the Bible in the present, or to transmit to the present the original Christian content given in history. They do not claim to be merely expressions of "a religion" or an "ethical ideal," which are not subject to any significant, theoretical discussion.[4] Such a description of them is false.

If systematic theology is to test whether a contemporary interpretation really can claim to be an interpretation, it must enter into a discussion with other sciences, especially philosophy. Bultmann has an advantage over Nygren in his recognition of this fact. He conceives of the biblical text as a call to men of today in contemporary preaching. If the interpretation is really to give expression to the gospel, the proclamation must encounter man's guilt, and the gospel must be a bestowal of righteousness over against the law. The reality of guilt is not dependent on the existence of scientifically "accurate" demands. Guilt exists without being supported by scientifically correct theories. This guilt is to be annulled (removed) by the

---

[4] "The special form in which religion claims validity consists in positing the transcendental reality of its object. But the transcendental-critical view remains in principle within the subjective sphere and leaves the question of a transcendental reality open and unanswered." (*Religious A Priori, op. cit.,* p. 149). *This* claim of the religious assertion (the object's transcendental reality) cannot be tested theoretically, and this is the only factor that Nygren considers. When, later on in his work in the history of thought, he deals with statements by various Christian authors, he regards these as religious statements. But these raise a different claim, a claim that can be tested. They claim to be interpretations of the first, the original, biblical propositions. The same claim is raised in the present by a number of contradictory assertions. If this claim cannot be tested when it is raised now in the present, nothing in the history of thought can be tested.

gospel. This is the point of conflict. Here the encounter must take place. But this is evidently not the place where the conflict between the Christian message and contemporary culture now occurs. It takes place at a number of other points. The gospel is, therefore, not conceived of as a gospel, but as a law in questions about doctrine.

Such a situation cannot be corrected unless theology openly discusses such questions as the truth of the New Testament miracles, the historical mistakes in the traditions of the origin of the books, etc. The whole problem of Bultmann's program of demythologizing is significant as an attempt to open this whole area for discussion. When that area has been entered, the communication between theology and other disciplines is open. It then becomes impossible for theology to shut itself up in its own room and engage in descriptions of religious propositions. It is the peculiar feature of Nygren's conception of theology that the relationship between philosophy and theology is at an end after philosophy has given theology "a scientific foundation." No Christian statement can be discussed because it is non-theoretical. But if the Christian assertion is an address to people in the present, a communication intended to collide at certain points with the estimate the hearer makes of himself, then the testing of this interpretation will force theology to consider a number of factors.

What we have said here makes clear our assumption that philosophy deals with the same material as theology, only from its own point of view. It implies that besides theology there is also a philosophy of religion working independently. What we deny is that the method of systematic theology can be determined by another discipline, philosophy of religion, philosophical ethics, or anything else. Philosophy of religion, as well as psychology and history of religion, work with the religious phenomenon as a whole. These disciplines have no obligation to expound the content of the Christian faith or the New Testament gospel. Church history is concerned with a definite material. It has to describe the history of the Christian church. (An investigation of a Buddhist fellowship is not church history but history of religion.) Exegesis is confined to a study of the Old and New Testaments. It takes into consideration whatever is necessary to elucidate these writings, but it does not arbitrarily examine any other religious documents. Then it, too, would become history of religion.

Systematic theology belongs among those disciplines which are bound to a certain material. The dependence on the material is relative. It appears only in comparison with philosophy, psychology, and history of religion, which deal with the religious phenomenon as a whole. But this relative dependence on the material must have at least one definite result: the method must be such that the material can be taken into consideration. This is the point we have been emphasizing during our whole presentation.

It is not reasonable that the method according to which a given content is to be interpreted should be determined before the encounter with that content takes place. When it has been possible to tie down theology in this manner, and when the theologians themselves have done this, the underlying reason for this procedure has been the feeling that theology lacks scientific prestige, and that we must secure this prestige for it. But such an attitude is not favorable to a realistic solution of any problem, least of all the problem of method. Generally the prestige is not enhanced by being subordinated to another magnitude which is supposed to enjoy prestige. It is far better to forget all about scientific prestige and to concentrate on this question: What areas of research are left when the other

167

disciplines have finished their work, and can these that are left be handled by ordinary, objective reasoning?

It then becomes apparent that these tasks of evaluation of the interpretations advanced in the past and in the present are left undone by the other disciplines. They are, however, essential tasks, and they can be pursued according to ordinary, objective reasoning. But in that case the bondage to a specific method appears as a mistake and a hindrance to a correct treatment of the content. If the task is to work with a certain content, the method has to be defined as we work with that content, not before that contact has been made. This implies an independence of philosophy when the method is being defined. But it implies also a full and free use of philosophy in the discussion of the problems raised by the content. In those cases where a philosophical argument determines the method of theology, the result is very often that the relationship ends at the point where the foundation has been laid. No further conversation takes place.

In this work we have given attention to the relationship of the gospel over against the law. There are other problems which complicate the evaluation of a given interpretation. Some of these we have touched upon from time to time in our presentation, others we have not even mentioned. These problems cannot be discussed abstractly. They must be considered as they appear during the analysis of the concrete content.

Index

169

Type used in this book
Body, 10 on 13 Janson; Display, Radiant
Paper: "R" Standard White Antique